The Handbook of Management Fads

Survival in business...
without taking yourself too seriously

The Handbook of Management Fads

Survival in business…
without taking yourself too seriously

Steve Morris

HAWKSMERE
A CRONER.CCH COMPANY

Published by the Hawksmere Group

12-18 Grosvenor Gardens

London SW1W 0DH.

www.hawksmere.co.uk

A CIP catalogue record for this book is available from the British Library.

ISBN 1 85418 077 0

Printed in Great Britain by MPG Books Limited, Bodmin.

The author

Steve Morris runs his own company providing management consultancy services specialising in publishing, training and development. He has worked extensively in the UK and abroad with blue-chip companies including Visa International, TSB, Lloyds, 3M and Shell International. He has a special interest in management practice and has written extensively on management related issues.

Thank you

I would like to thank the Burton Morris team who worked with me on this book. Phil Rigg added some cool elan to a dangerously over-heating text. Graham Willcocks added lots of words, a lot of the wisdom and some good jokes. It's because others were involved in the book that I sometimes lapse into the Royal We.

Contents

3

4

5

6

7

What's your affliction?

1

Not again or words to that effect

Recently I was speaking to a manager – not a gnarled old seen-it-all-before manager, but a comparative spring chicken. In just a few years this manager had experienced a heady cocktail of TQM, Downsizing, Performance Related Pay and Outsourcing. Now he'd been called into his manager's office to be told that the UK arm of the company had just been told to try JR by its American parent.

His first reaction was the time-honoured, *Not Again.* He was suffering from fad shock syndrome – a mortifying cynicism and weariness about the value and application of management fads. He isn't alone. All of us have trod the fad trail so often, so far and so frequently that it is wearing thin. We've heard the stuttering excuses for fads gone wrong, for direction changes, for new bunches of management consultants being brought in to solve the problems the last lot left. We've seen some of the carnage fads can cause – a customer care initiative in the wrong hands is more potent than a exocet with a bad sense of humour.

His next reaction was to pause and ask… what is JR?

A fad is born

His boss looked at him for a moment and then she told him.

JR stands for Job Revitalisation. It's a technique for raising motivation and output that is currently sweeping across Europe, having been immensely successful in South East Asia. This in itself makes it interesting – the very fact that it did not start in the USA but in one of the emerging and vibrant economies of the Pacific rim. If it's good in Taiwan it must be good here.

The principles are deceptively simple and the process was documented in 1995 by A.T. Chen-Wah of PulPuhjon University School of Management. In fact it was his extremely successful book (summarised in an article in the Harvard Business News in December 1996) which led to the explosion in JR.

Professor Chen-Wah was commissioned by the KLB Consumer Electronics Group in 1990, to do two things. He was to identify reasons for the significant decline in productivity over the past two years and was also to propose ways of reversing the trend.

He researched human potential and satisfaction amongst 14,980 workers doing the more mundane jobs that exist in many manufacturing environments in South East Asia. His discovery was that, as recently as ten years ago simply having a job with KLB was seen as a mark of social success and carried status and worth in the community. But this had changed and by the time he started his work over 38% of manual (skilled and semi-skilled) workers in the electronics manufacturing and assembly industries were expressing either significant or serious dissatisfaction with their employment.

The problem was not linked to traditional views of job satisfaction that relate to the intrinsic rewards of the work itself. It was more related to the issue of the status of a particular job role, in the eyes of the community and one's peers.

Chen-Wah turned to the approaches devised decades ago by Frederick Herzberg and other motivation experts. These have stood the test of time and have become received wisdom in employee motivation, so he explored ways of using job redesign to add some interest and satisfaction to the roles. He changed some parts of different jobs round, added some new tasks and gave people new things to do. While expecting success to follow fairly quickly, he was amazed to find that his trial of traditional job redesign failed miserably.

The breakthrough came with the realisation that two key issues were central here. One was that what mattered was not the reality but the perception. Debriefing interviews with the employees showed that the issue was less about the direct satisfaction achieved from the work, and more about status and perceived value and image. The other was that the employee themselves did not have control of the job redesign process, so empowerment was not taking place.

Perceptions of status

Giving an employee more responsibility without formalising the process did not allow them to claim status and recognition. Some formal recognition – almost some form of ceremony was needed so that the employee could have some sort of badge, or rite of passage to show tangibly that the employer valued them by giving them difficult tasks to do, by stretching them and expecting more of them. Without such a ritual, performance would not rise as markedly as was needed.

In some ways there are parallels with the motivational 'trick' of giving someone a more important title, with no more money or responsibility. This was the flash of inspiration. What if that status issue was really what motivated people, in today's material and status-conscious world? What if Herzberg, MacGregor, Maslow and all the other motivational gurus had been right about the time they were describing, but had been looking at a totally different work environment and social structure from that which was emerging in the late twentieth century?

In other words, had Chen-Wah's failure given a clue to a way of bringing motivation up to date for the new millennium? He believed so, and devised JR to test out his new theories. The results were astounding, from a process that differs only slightly from what has gone before.

The Job Revitalisation process extends traditional job redesign. Each employee is eligible for JR only after two years' successful employment. The key to the status element is that at the end of two years they must turn in a performance evaluation that shows them to meet the required standard for entry to JR. Thereafter, each year's review must meet the required standard or they cannot carry out a JR review in that year. So someone in the JR programme is instantly recognisable as someone with success and status. They even get overalls with JR monogrammed on the top pocket.

Status plus empowerment

Status is crucial but the other factor – allowing employees to take control – was also vital. The JR programme consists of an annual review where each employee identifies tasks outside their current role which they wish to undertake and which would be most challenging to them. They also specify which of their current tasks have become mundane.

Each employee then (with their nominated JR mentor acting as facilitator) trades a task with a colleague. So each individual exchanges at least one main task with another worker – based on the notion that what has become easy (and possibly boring) for one person after two years is a new challenge for someone who has not yet done it.

In the first year this exchange is contained within the section in which the employees work. The employees themselves have the right to make the trade – management cannot stop them and it is the employees who carry the can for any failures.

In the second year the exchange takes place across section boundaries, so an employee in, say, TV assembly, can exchange a task from a colleague in calculator calibration. Each is responsible for training their counterpart and remains available as a consultant should they be needed.

In the third and subsequent years it is possible to trade tasks across departments, so someone in production can exchange tasks with someone in marketing – if an exchange can be arranged.

Results have been astounding. The motivation that comes from new tasks is supplemented by the fact that each employee is in charge of his or her own destiny at work. The improvement in output starts from day one, as employees strive to achieve the performance levels required for entry to the prestigious JR programme. It then continues as they regularly have new challenges and learning experiences to handle, as part of a process which carries prestige and status.

Three things then emerge from this look at Job Revitalisation. First, it is merely an extension of the traditional job redesign techniques known by all HR managers. Second, it contains a simple but powerful motor that drives the concept. Third, it's a load of twaddle that we made up in about twelve minutes!

There is no such thing as JR – although the really scary thing is that there easily could be if we decided to launch it as a scam on an unsuspecting business world. Somebody would buy it – and would buy our consultancy services to implement it – if we packaged it right.

Not long ago there was a school of management thought that said 'If it ain't broke, don't fix it'. At the same time someone described the concept of Business Process Re-engineering, which one cynic summarised as 'If it ain't broke… break it'.

So who's right? What can we believe? What do we do about fads?

Let's get one thing straight. Effective and efficient management is one of the most important issues ever. We like management. It is fascinating, wonderfully refreshing and a source of immense interest. We believe in good management and we believe that management is fun. There can be nothing more creative than coming up with new ideas about organisations and how to manage the people in them and there is also a need to continually refresh the language of management. So we have no problem with management thinking.

Our aim is not to rubbish any of the great management thinkers. Indeed, these are the very people we admire and for whom we feel sorry. They came up with what now seem like simple and obvious ideas and concepts – the ones we all take for granted in organisations. But at the time their thinking was novel and revolutionary and it is only because their ideas have become accepted as fact (or at least highly probable theories) that we have lost sight of the fact that someone actually had to invent the notion of motivation, management style or quality management. Our sadness for them is because it is their often brilliant ideas that have been hi-jacked and turned into fads.

However in this book we have decided not to toe the party line. We're not out to defend anyone and while we aren't going to throw out good ideas we have decided to call a fad a fad. We shall call downsizing indiscriminate sacking and retribution, and name TQM as a source of enough hot air to fill a Richard Branson balloon. And fads have their victims amongst the people in the organisation, as well as in the ranks of management thinkers.

So if you've trod the fad road and had enough ...read on.

Why enter the dragon's lair?

You may wonder why we wrote this book. We could say that there is a current fad for knocking fads... but that's a bit too cynical, even for us.

The answer is that it came from our enquiring minds and a genuine interest in the 'where are they now' stakes. We have been asked over the years to write books and articles on all sorts of management techniques... most of which seemed to sink without trace.

So one reason for writing it was to apologise to the world on behalf of clever management experts... you know, the people who take a perfectly sound notion and turn it into a fad. We happen to care about you and the people around you, as you struggle to implement the impossible. It's not fair for someone to ask what you think of the Emperor's New Clothes, so we decided to come out with it and admit that he's naked, most of the time.

Another reason is to work out where they all are now. While quality is obviously vital, what exactly did happen to Quality Circles? While knowing what we're here to achieve is critical, where is management by objectives today? And the team briefing model…? Is anyone still implementing sound principles under the disguise of these threadbare old war-horses?

It looks like a duck

A past president of the USA is credited with saying that if it walks like a duck, looks like a duck, quacks, swims and lays eggs… maybe it's a duck. In other words, sometimes the obvious is what it is.

So some of those old fads are still around. But not necessarily as fads – more as simple common-sense approaches that would have been tried anyway. And only by people who really understand what they are looking at. The basic problem with fads is that they suffer from Chinese Whispers. There is a sound message there at the start, but it gets changed, added to and refined out of all recognition as it passes down the line.

It's like JR. Plain and simple common sense tells us that it's in everyone's interest for people to enjoy their work. Yet we rely on someone else to come up with a label for it and to stick it on a potted and simplified formula.

So we end up not with the main message but an altered set of instructions, a quick fix approach to a problem that can't be solved or that didn't exist in the first place.

One of the most important and telling moments in our lives as consultants was when we stood in front of a group of very senior executives who had come to hear us tell them how to manage change. Well, that's not quite true; they hadn't originally come to hear us but the person they were expecting had been left on the platform in Manchester when the train timetable changed without notice. (There's a moral in there, somewhere!)

Anyway, we started by saying that we were sorry, but the topic they had paid to talk about was not valid. Managing change was a contradiction in terms. It was, we said, a bit like trying to knit fog – a great idea but totally impossible.

Our opening tenet was that change is simply unmanageable. It's not like a burger bar or a budget. Change is a concept that involves people and their emotions. All the books on it say that if you tell people in time, involve them, get their commitment and all this stuff, you can manage change. It needs careful planning but great managers handle change as easily as scoffing an ice cream… according to the books by writers who have often never managed anything. This notion of change as a process we can control was absolutely wrong, we contended. Absolute nonsense. Change is a force with a mind of its own – sent from outside the universe to try the patience of all managers and every human being. You can't manage electricity, wind, or the tides. It's not on to try and control the weather. You can understand them, forecast what might happen, work with them and minimise the damage they can cause, but you cannot manage them.

Then we asked a simple question. How many people in this room (out of about 60) believe they must be doing something wrong and are failures compared to the rest of the audience – because they can't manage change when all the books say all good managers can do it? At first, all eyes were cast down at the conference programmes…

then a few hooded glances shot round the room between those present. Then one tentative hand went up… then a couple more, and then a whole forest. Eventually a huge round of applause swelled and exploded and in the calm that followed someone stood up and said that they had just heard the most valuable statement about managing change that they had ever encountered. It was all right not to be able to do everything the text books said. It was all right not to feel guilty because they could not do what the books said.

These people had felt as if they – individually – were failing; as if they were the only ones in the room who could not do it, when everyone else obviously could. And all because the text books say that we can manage change when all we can really do is limit the damage, control the failure and cope with the process that threatens 99% of the population? All because a book said it was right and someone who claims to be an expert said this is the way to do it.

It's sad to think that we could then have started a fad – a Living With Change Because You Can't Manage It fad. But what is really creepy is that it could well have become the flavour of that year! It would have sunk into oblivion by now, but it could have had its brief and glorious moment.

A third reason for writing this book is that management fads are rather like embarrassing teenage photographs. These days you may look cool and respectable but just think in the 70s you were probably all knitted tank tops, flares and inappropriate haircuts. Perhaps just a few years ago you may have been evangelising about Just in Time, or SPC or the like. And perhaps when you think back you feel a bit silly about getting carried away by all that hot air and the dubious promises. Perhaps you remained unashamed for now.

So, this book is about all our yesterdays. It paints the picture in all its crummy detail. Some of it is nostalgic, some plain angry – but from it we hope emerges a picture of the exciting, fresh, frustrating, messed up world of management thinking.

Why do we need management fads?

Some cynics would say, to provide a home for venerable old senior managers turned freelance management consultants, stateless academics from bad universities trying to make an extra buck and others too downright disreputable to mention.

But we wouldn't say that.

Some people would argue that it's the Jones syndrome – keeping up with the competition. One point of view is that the firm down the road is a good firm and they employ all graduates… therefore we ought to employ all graduates because we want to be a good firm, too.

This is as flawed as the logic that says that dogs, cats and marmosets have four legs and are mammals; I am a mammal therefore I have four legs. The fact that the firm down the road is a biotechnical laboratory and we are a pizzeria ought to have some relevance to the equation.

We would say there is some of this, but there is more to it.

Fads actually plug into a basic human need. We need to believe that there is an answer to everything. We need to feel that everything would be fine at work if only we knew a bit more, or did a bit more, or made some changes. And there are some very credible people and theories out there to help persuade us.

It's our own insecurity that leads us to accept other people's ideas. Like managing change, we cannot bring ourselves to believe that maybe we do know, we do understand and we are right. Surely someone else must know more than we do, so we must take their word for it.

There's another more basic point, too. It's us that buys the fads – it's our insecurity that drives us to need the designer labels. Behind the best-selling book that launches a new fad there's a simple idea. We often would benefit from the little gem that sits at their heart, but what starts out as a sound and sensible nugget of an idea or concept somehow gets hijacked along the way.

Take something like customer care. It's been around for hundreds of years. My grandfather – who had a small grocer's shop – used to say to me that the customer was always right. Now, half a century later (and probably more than that because I'm sure his father told him – and he didn't invent the concept) writers, consultants and gurus are telling us that customers are important. Tom Peters made a fortune out of it – and he's right! The fascinating thing is that we nod sagely – as if the scales are falling from our eyes as we speak.

But we know that customers matter. We may have forgotten it in the maelstrom of consumerism… but we know that without customers we don't have a business. After all, aren't we customers and don't we matter? It's so obvious it's as if we must have missed the point and are out of a secret that everyone else knows. So we nod, go along with it and pretend to see the Emperor's New Clothes.

It's just that the fad industry is always on the lookout for an old idea to update and make fashionable.

Take the following example.

The author of this book went to buy a ticket for a railway journey just the other Sunday. One window was open in the ticket booth. A queue of 19 people had formed. Your ever smiling author had a train to catch in 20 minutes. The minutes ticked away and your author noticed an employee was sitting at another window in the booth doing some paperwork. He walked up to the man and enquired whether it would be possible to open the window and take some money for a ticket because trains were about to be missed.

The employee looked up, surprised.

'No mate. I'm (hacked) off with having to tell you people that it ain't me. He said. I'm not tickets today. Now you've lost your place in the queue, too!'

One response to this experience is to write and complain to the senior management. Another is to cause a scene, and to stand and shout about how simply bloody awful some people are at looking after customers. A third one is to mutter under our breath and accept that this is how things are – and that's the normal approach.

But the faddist would come up with a technique to suit this situation. Every company in the country would be exhorted to train its staff, in teams, so that Management through Understanding became de rigeur. The trick is to talk sympathetically to the staff member who was rude and then run loads of training sessions that allow all staff to perceive the experience as if they were customers. They are then encouraged to project the implications of that onto the back-cloth of business success and see just how much impact that one tiny situation has on the profits of a train company. It's like chaos theory, where a butterfly flapping its wings in the Amazon basin causes a flood in Switzerland.

On the other hand, of course, we could just sack the obnoxious jerk that is always rude to customers, or discipline him – once we have tried training and awareness raising as a fair first line of attack.

Generally, when companies are this messed up some bushy tailed person in the marketing or strategy department decides to look for an elixir to make things better.

Perhaps it is a very British and American thing. It is said (we're not sure by whom) that it is only the British and the Americans who pin their hope on celebrity economists. These economists have come to be more important than planned rational approaches. We are looking for the one guy who can give us the one answer. Not surprisingly, the economists haven't delivered.

But any decent person is interested in the New – and fads are all about the new and what the future can offer.

Also, fads are exciting. There is a real buzz when you get caught up in implementing your first fad. Rather like in the spirit of the Blitz, everyone pulls together, everyone has a role towards the greater good and the enemies are those who resist the change, who don't want to play ball.

But we sometimes wonder how much the fads really add. Let's give you an example.

Half a century ago, the chief executive of 3M wrote down what he believed the company was, and should be, based on.

'*Those men and women to whom we delegate authority and responsibility, if they are good people, are going to want to do their jobs in their own way.*'

Just note this. It encapsulates a simple view of motivation, delegation, empowerment, creativity, innovation and the like – whole areas where sackloads of twaddle have been written about since.

And by the way the same chief executive said:

'*If people are any good they will make mistakes, but we should welcome this because mistakes are essential for growth.*'

This visionary was heralding all sorts of modern stuff about learning organisations and the like. Or, he was simply saying what he thought.

And when you see the simplicity, yet all-encompassing nature of the vision you wondered why we ever needed management fads. Surely 3M got it right all those years ago and any company that did as 3M did wouldn't need any help from a guru or dream-maker.

Might as well pack up and go home? Not quite.

Fear and loathing

In his demented book *Fear and Loathing in Las Vegas,* Hunter S Thompson comments that the defining moment of the 1960s came when the Beatles consulted the Maharishi Mahesh Yogi: this sounded the death-knell of 60s idealism. The decade's icons had sought the guidance of a 'guru', a spiritual teacher whose expertise in wisdom, in the theory and practice of life, was supposedly superior to theirs. The pursuit of beauty and happiness was, for Thompson, incompatible with gurus of whatever persuasion.

Why indeed bother with gurus? Can they really do anything for anyone but themselves? Does an 'expert' necessarily have anything to say? And if they have authority – who anointed them in the caste? Should you defer to *that* person's judgement too? Or is the belief in another's prescription the mark of slavishness, moral corruption and decadence?

Thompson thought so, and he was not alone: the view has been articulated by psychiatrist R D Laing and, before him, by Nietzsche's anti-Christ figure, Zarathustra. One can imagine Zarathustra standing on the mountain and, instead of laying down the tablets of the law, turning to his disciples and screaming:

'Do not follow me – this is my way! You must find your own!'

How do *you* feel about experts and professionals, leaders and gurus? Do you have faith in them, or do you mistrust panaceas? Do you trust your own judgement, or do you think it's safer and more sensible to be led? Do you *find your own way* – or do you, like the faddists in this book, warm to the words of the guru, recite his mantra, and follow meekly in his footsteps?

An anatomy
of fiddle-faddles

2

Fad spotting for beginners

What makes a fad a fad? How do we identify our subject in action? What distinguishes a fad from other, worthier concepts and practices?

The word 'fad', first of all, derives from the 19th century term *fiddle-faddle*, which referred to the aimless movements of the violin-player's or fiddler's elbow. So when we refer to 'management fads' ourselves, we're talking loosely about managerial frivolity – management *crazes*.

With such inscrutable terms of reference and such an array of fads to consider, let's adopt an Aristotelian method. For the time being, we will simply describe some examples of managerial frivolity that we have actually witnessed – then, later, we may be able to identify meaningful patterns, make inferences, and perhaps lay down some firmer judgements.

The fad life cycle

Here, then, is a typical day in the life-cycle of a fad.

An idea appears. Perhaps it makes its first appearance as a speculative article in an obscure periodical; perhaps it's a case study in a management journal written by an unusually reflective manager; perhaps it's a one-off piece of analysis by a consultant or a partner; perhaps it's a melodramatic think-piece by a jobbing Texan university professor called Franklin Tripleburger T. Schwartz, Jr.

Then a journalist writes about it. The next step is for the idea to be challenged. Then, gathering steam as it goes, it suddenly, rapidly, begins to look like an accepted wisdom.

More heat is generated – in fact, soon there's a whole body of literature generated by people who've never read the primary text on the topic. By this time, no-one is quite sure where it originally came from anyway. Only one person has ever read the relevant text, and this innocent messenger has long since been buried face-down in the avalanche. Counter-claims and accusations are made; a catchy name is invented to encapsulate the fad – like Job Revitalisation. (Incidentally, as you'll see later, it is crucial that the name can be summarised in a set of initials, ideally three initials, that run trippingly off the tongue.)

Hastily-drafted books are written. Semi-digested theories are elaborated confidently (and smugly). Management consultants contest them. At any given moment no-one is quite sure who knows what, and whether there was anything substantial to grasp in the first place. No matter. Meaningful insignia or badges begin to appear on puffed-up chests – Q for Quality, perhaps. The fad is by now being implemented – tested out – on real human beings!

(A feature of the best fads is that, when they are in full swing, unbelieving voices are simply not heard. It's sacrilege to utter the blasphemous words *'This…idea… is… nonsense!'* Just as some mental illnesses are characterised by the sufferer's sense of absolute clarity and certainty, so with the fad an unreal consensus prevails in which everyone hymns together the Unquestionable Truth of the One Holy Fiddle-Faddle.)

But the wheel is now beginning to turn . A dissenting voice is heard. The dissident attacks the fad in an article. The company most clearly associated with the fad goes broke. The theorist who wrote the original, humble article appears – and officially disowns the theory.

A few sad remnants of the fad remain, and a few latecomers still champion it, even now. At this stage, oddly, the public sector starts to implement it. But interest in the theory is dying out…

A new fad appears and replaces the old one. New badges appear on old chests. It's all over. So farewell then, fiddle-faddle.

It is at this stage that managers in government departments start adopting the fad.

Faddish language

Part and parcel of the Fad Phenomenon is a new and occasionally infuriating vocabulary. Sometimes this language of fads is fun – native speakers of English can now be heard singing the praises of brand *leverage* (pronounced the American way, to rhyme with *beverage*) and also process *re-routing* (pronounced to rhyme with *spouting*). But often it's merely pretentious and obscure.

For a time, UK business talk was peppered with references to *kaizen*, the famous Japanese management concept of, er…what was it? It's difficult not to smile at such a heroic attempt to dignify the banal by associating it with the exotic, but the effect of such pretentious coinages is to undermine the language of management, and in the end, to discredit the idea of management itself.

Competencies is one we really love! Competence, yes, as a concept. But competencies??

Listen out in the staff toilets for other awkward and exclusive phrases in current circulation. Try not to let any sniggers escape from the cubicle as you overhear the likes of:

- We're so snowed under – this is my first comfort break of the day

- I'm determined that we all sing from the same hymn sheet

- Leveraging brand equities is what keeps me excited

- Let's take a walk in the woods on this idea

- I want to run a few ideas up the flagpole to see what you think

- She was jetlagged, so she's gone for a power nap

- I'm so impressed at your ability to think outside the box…

- …but sadly you've made the mistake of thinking outside the envelope

- We were shocked – it was a total 68-ton gorilla for us

And, from the 'quality movement':

- We must achieve conformance on this point!

- Continuous improvement is my philosophy – and of course the need to ensure product integrity…

The problem isn't what the words say – there's nothing better than getting it right first time, every time – but the way that the meaning is lost to the incantation of this meaningless mantra. People like Crosby and Deming (look them up) really knew about quality, but they made the mistake of writing down the odd phrase that comes back to haunt and trivialise the whole movement. Fitness for purpose… right first time… survival is not compulsory, and so on.

Evangelism comes in many forms, so admit it – are you one of the converts to this exotic, mysterious, and downright *fiddle-faddly* new religion?

The elements

So the elements of a fad. Well there is a guru – a leader, who explains and perpetuates the ideas. There are followers, disciples who evangelise and spread the message – keeping the fire alight. There is a literature of the fad – often sketchy. There are slogans and language to accompany the fad.

Above all there is an answer… or at least the promise of an answer because another company made it work for them.

There are always firms of consultants and university departments in search of cash, who spread the word that this is the greatest idea ever. They run seminars and symposia, invite speakers from large companies who say all the right things about how great this fad has been for them and their organisation.

The consultants know about the fad and how it can really produce the goods. They can help implement it for you. They are the ones you need to employ.

So you do, they don't and the whole thing slows down just a little. You start to get slightly sweaty palms… this is not all going quite as well as you had been led to believe. But it is early days and they are the experts. Throw a bit more money at it and it will be all right.

Then things start to go decidedly pear-shaped. It doesn't quite stick, the impetus drops away and everyone quietly forgets about it. The consultants disappear from the scene and nobody in the organisation makes a great song and dance because they invited these people in. To make a fuss would draw attention to their own judgement, so maybe it's best to stay silent and keep one's head down.

And then... it's on to the next fad.

Varieties of fiddle

When the faddist scans an organisation looking for something to hypothesise about, there are several possible areas of intervention. In general terms, you can examine the physical work environment – usually the office space itself; alternatively, you can turn your attention to the work process – the product or information chains which lead to an output; or, again, you can focus on the people themselves who do the job, the 'human resources' (as they're now faddishly known). This last leans towards the science of psychology, trying to understand the nature of motivation and to increase the emotional and material satisfaction of individuals and teams, so as to make the company more successful. Let's now look at these three areas more closely and ask why so many faddists spend so much time scrutinising and dribbling over them.

1. The work environment

The workplace is, in a sense, company psychology made visible. How you stand in relation to your colleagues is often expressed in the layout of the office space, and in the relation of a particular office to the building.

Traditional models of organisation made no bones about physical structure and its psychological force. The 19th century Utilitarian Jeremy Bentham designed a prison in which all inmates could be seen serving their time from a single power-centred vantage point. His aptly-named 'Panopticon' demonstrated schematically – and brutally – to the visitor exactly who was in charge. Ruthlessly paring down the institution's ratio of staff to inmates, it satisfied the minimal supervisory requirements of the time at basic cost. It also betrayed a terrifying megalomania.

Large modern companies often dance as clumsily in their concrete office blocks. A well-known London construction firm owns a multi-storey building in which its employees are layered, from first to tenth floor, according (with the odd discrepancy) to their rank and status. As you make your way up the company staircase, you pass through the post room and the lowly clerical staff, up through the more professional layers of draughtspeople and middle managers, through to the 'client floor', the project and senior managers. These elusive characters are known to the rank-and-file mostly by their initials alone. They walk on a different quality of carpet. If you ever wanted to see a demoralised workforce which knows it is cheap, dispensable and insecure, you would need to look no further than the ground floor workers in this building.

Faddists have inevitably tried to re-think this messy business. Their ideas have mostly aimed at making offices more like home, introducing scatter-cushions, soft lighting and even beds. They have also tried to reorganise office space for reasons of cost, sharing a single desk between two employees when schedules allow. The possibilities of new office design are often constrained by pre-existing buildings, but there's still scope for architects and faddists to work together on this one. Growing awareness of environmental issues is bound to have an impact – The Ark, an astounding boat-shaped office building in West London designed by a Swedish architect, is perhaps an early herald of this trend. We might well see a much more radical reshaping of the work-space in the years to come.

2. The work process

Once you've seen past the office or production space itself, the next thing to examine might be the process – the way in which information is handled, products are assembled or whatever. If the business process deploys workers on a factory-line, faddists might fancy speeding it up, slowing it down, automating it, or increasing the number of line-workers. They might suggest storing fewer or more materials, training more exacting or less exacting supervisors, or taking longer or shorter tea-breaks.

Businesses in the modern market fear losing touch with their customers. This concern leads to huge market research budgets, sales and marketing materials written and designed with specific customers in mind' and other projects designed to 'keep the company listening at the front line'. Faddists, of course, have a lot to say about these systems – how to streamline them, how to identify weak areas, how to stop them from interfering with your customer communications.

'Systems and processes' (says the faddist) 'need to be customer-led and customer-driven'. (Here they sigh and produce a lengthy report full of swinging cuts and organisational reshuffles.)

'We'll show you how to do it.'

3. The people

It's perhaps easiest to see what there is to be gained from studying people, their individual behaviours, beliefs and modes of interaction. More and more companies recognise that their most valuable asset is their human resources – and that without a well-trained, well-motivated, well-remunerated and well-appreciated workforce they are inviting failure at every level, internal and external.

Individuals need to see why they're doing what they do each day and how it fits into the wider company system and strategy. They also need to be able to use their initiative; make decisions and exercise some control over their day's activities; receive support and guidance from colleagues when needed; make mistakes without being punished for it; and so on.

Without attending to these crucial aspects of psychology, individuals might just as well resign themselves to the traditional worker's mind-set caricatured by Tony Hancock – the feeling of being a faceless cog in the machine, uninterested in your work, loathing your colleagues, and shrinking from your manager as a Victorian schoolchild shrank in fear from his rod-wielding beadle.

Enter the faddist.

New ways of appraising performance are suggested, new ways of offering remuneration. New styles of relationship are envisaged, and new means of achieving them – mufti days, assertiveness, outward-bound activities, training courses – with the aim of helping you relax, communicate better, learn more, bond with colleagues, teamwork more efficiently… You are supposed to appraise your manager, appraise yourself, improve your weaknesses, work to your strengths…

Fiddling with environments

3

Some real fads

So let's dip our toes in the water and look at some real fads. To begin with fads that tinker around with where we work – our work space.

Before you read on take a look around you. Has your office been the victim of an environmental fad? If you worked in our office you'd probably wished it had – we tend to be pretty basic around these parts.

Are your desks arranged in a conventional way or plain weird? Do you have your own desk? Have you been open planned?

Read on.

1. Hot desking and hotelling

Yes… there really are fads called these names.

In response to the sky-high cost of office space in Manhattan and Tokyo, certain companies saw an opportunity to save themselves money. How could all that expensive floor space simply be left unoccupied when people were away from the office? What waste. What down-time. What dollar bills slowly being burned.

Why pay full-time rates for space that was only being used intermittently by the increasing cohorts of external consultants coming and going? Why allow staff the luxury of their own desks?

The solution was a spot of *hot desking,* or *hotelling* as it was sometimes known: the idea that several workers would share a single desk. External consultants, as well as full-time employees, would have to book their desks in the same way as they would reserve a restaurant table. So, if a manager had an appointment on Tuesday from 11am to 3pm, she would have to book her desk from, say, 7.30 to 10.30am and then again from, say, 3.30pm to 8.00pm, when she could finally crawl to the bar and discuss tomorrow's business.

A sublime refinement of this scheme came when some companies set up storage cupboards into which the contents of each employee's desk would be shoved. Then, ten minutes before the employee returned to the reserved desk, staff would carefully arrange on the desktop the appropriate pens, documents, flowers, wedding photographs and toys. This desk-rota would continue throughout the day, with staff carefully clearing and re-setting the desk according to the day's Desk Appointments book.

As fads go, it was spectacularly fiddly. Paying administrative staff to act like waiters seemed (paradoxically, given the initial motivation) expensive and inefficient. Why not instead pay staff to work directly on primary work tasks, and let productivity pay for desk down-time? Perhaps in central Manhattan – hey! – prohibitive office rental rates really did call for radical organisational measures. But hot-desking in Aberystwyth and Slough?

The craze had unforeseen destabilizing effects on office environments, reflecting a deepening lack of security in the wider labour market and distressing employees with a daily reminder of their dispensability. If it was no longer possible to refer to '*my* desk', was it still possible to refer to '*my* office', '*my* company' or '*my* job'?

The scheme also highlighted the question of mutual respect between employees and employers: was it honourable and decent to sweep away a person's possessions or worktools the moment they left their desk, or was it rather inhuman and demoralising? Many felt the policy had an alienating effect, and judging by the fad's fate, managers agreed.

2. Romping

If you come into your office one morning to discover the desks have all been thrown out and your manager is asking you to Romp, don't jump out of the window.

You might have assumed the hot-desking fad had come and gone; Romping is like hot desking plus mufti. It's the *Revolutionary Office Mobility Programme*. The aim is to recreate the office space to be more flexible, user-friendly and enjoyable. One company based in Birmingham, for instance, have thrown out 90% of their desks to set up Romping spaces with sofas. Now you move around, working in a different space next to different members of the team each day, inviting and stimulating new ideas.

3. One desking

As the name implies one desking is where the organisation has just the one desk – a very very long desk, but just the one nonetheless.

The logic works this way.

Our organisation should work as a team. Our office space means we work as individuals. Why not make one enormous desk and we all work together – forming in teams around the desk as appropriate.

Sounds great?

Try to get some peace and quiet, try to keep things organised, try to have a meeting with some customers, try to phone a loved one during the day.

Great for design and advertising agencies but not for real people.

4. The total environment

Starting from the premise that your average office space does nothing to foster creativity – on the contrary, in fact – what about changing it into a congenial area which is really conducive to working effectively?

Adopted by interior decorating and design consultancies as well as other professional agencies on the creative side, the 'total environment' movement set its heart on making the workplace a home-from-home, shunning the traditional image of work as an unpleasant activity and single-mindedly creating a welcoming haven – a cross between a bower of bliss and a boudoir.

The impulse was to refashion the office. The result, however, was to create somewhat cultish organisations having:

- no desks – but comfy sofas with big lights
- no staff canteens – but gourmet restaurants serving sumptuous dishes
- no clear knocking-off time – but beds with huge comfy quilts.

In the lobbies-cum-sanctuaries, for those in need of inspiration, were oases complete with palm trees. The tinkle of artificially-pumped water would permeate the studio. Underneath the palm trees you could either clear your mind in readiness for the next brainstorm or nestle up with a client – removing your open-toed sandals first – to talk business.

What effect did this total environment have on its devotees?

It had a literal effect: it *became* their total environment. They would choose not to leave the office because it supplanted home in so many ways. Often combined with a design-, space- and/or human resource-based fad (empowerment, for example), it exerted a quite tyrannical grip on many individuals in the creative field. It also encouraged a pernicious rash of long hours and workaholism, and was accused by some observers of being deliberately manipulative – ironically, the opposite of its initial intention.

Comfort is one thing, but employees did not really want companies to fashion a version of their ideal domestic habitat for working purposes – certainly not when it conjured up a sort of cloying, pseudo-family atmosphere which colleagues were somehow supposed to share.

The total environment, like many other ostensibly freedom-promoting fads, was in the end deemed by many of its original advocates to be superficial and oppressive.

Fiddling with processes

4

Fiddling with the office environment is bad enough – but what about fiddling around with the very way we work? There's a lot of it about.

Pareto analysis

Sometimes referred to as ABC or concentration analysis, this holds that 80 per cent of a goal can be achieved with only 20 per cent of the effort required to achieve 100 per cent of the goal.

Pareto was a late-19th century empirical philosopher and economist who had some wacky ideas on income distribution, seeing the economy as a self-regulating organism with its own laws, and deducing that voluntary human intervention could therefore do nothing to structurally affect it.

He also developed the law of 'the trivial many and the critical few', which divides items like stock levels, sales and customers into three groups in order to identify the 'critical 20 per cent'. This can then be concentrated on (hence 'concentration analysis').

In fiddly-faddly circles, Pareto's name is bandied around loosely to mean 'you can get *almost everything* – with *relatively* little effort'. Random examples include:

- 80 per cent of your sales volume is generated by 20 per cent of customers

- 20 per cent of your friends account for 80 per cent of your bad debts

- 80 per cent of the Pareto principle can be understood with 20 per cent of the effort required to care about it

That's your twenty. Now judge for yourself whether you've still got 80 per cent for the full Pareto, or whether you'd rather save it for the next fad.

From just-in-time to just-in-case

One case at a time.

'Just-in-time' was a management concept originally developed in the Japanese car industry. It was applied to factory lines, dividing up the production process into a sequence of small units so that each unit could deliver to the next exactly what was needed to carry out the next manufacturing step. At the end of each day, each unit receives precisely what it will need for tomorrow's production; the supply chain requires a uniform demand at all points along the production line.

The whole system obviously relies on extremely rigorous delivery timetabling but when it works, costly stockpiling and machine down-times are minimised. When it doesn't work, units have no materials to work with, cannot therefore provide what the next unit along needs, and the opposite of efficient production occurs – i.e. breakdown.

Interestingly, and unlike the conventional manufacturing process where the product is 'pushed' from the beginning of the factory line to the end, JIT is classically 'pulled' from the end of the line: Worker A is only *allowed* to do her work when Worker B is ready for it. The system only works well for conventional mass-produced factory products – it is less useful for job shop operations (turbines or jet engine production, for example) where perhaps only one or two units a week are produced.

'Just-in-case' is a case of adjusting 'just-in-time'. In other words, it's a corrective to the last-minute, on-the-button approach, which is highly efficient – until it breaks down.

Operating 'just-in-time' management across a relatively small region like Japan is one thing, where external deliveries were stepped up from weekly to daily to hourly as JIT was refined. But guaranteeing deliveries to very tight schedules across the American vastness was quite another challenge. So 'just-in-case' was introduced as an insurance. A limited degree of stock-holding, formerly held to be a waste of money, was introduced as a sensible and efficient response to the flaws of just-in-time management.

To the fadologist, the modification of Japanese *just-in-time* is a superb illustration of *kaizen* in action.

Re-engineering

This is a movement of the 1990s. Its authors say that this is not a quick fix or an instant solution. But they do hint that other people have hijacked their concepts and turned them into fads, products and services.

The basis of business process re-engineering is that companies at the end of the twentieth century are still working to tasks that were appropriate a couple of hundred years ago. Whereas Adam Smith broke down work into small and manageable tasks, that was right for then. Nowadays what is needed is a total rethink.

Processes rather than concepts should be the focus – a process being any group of actions or activities which add value for the customer. And the message is that organisations should not keep on tinkering with the edges of the old processes, but should start again from scratch. Today's needs are not met by yesterday's arrangements.

Companies should ask themselves not 'how can we do this better/cheaper/more easily' or 'can we make this faster?'. The questions are: 'Why do we do any of this? Do we need to? Should we be doing something entirely different?'

Chaos theory

This is not the chaos theory so analytically (and eloquently) set out by James Gleich in his best-selling book *CHAOS: Making a New Science*, though there is some connection.

Gleich's account starts in the 1960s, when early computer scientists began to model weather systems. Their aim was to enable precise long-term prediction, but the project turned out to be impossible: simple low-level changes in the system cascaded upwards into complex and unpredictable effects. The butterfly's wing fluttering today in Beijing could transform weather systems months later in New York. Small scales and large scales, however, interacted at apparently random points to produce a kind of chaotic order – a law of chaos.

Chaos theory is subtle and resists quick exposition, but suffice to say that it has profoundly affected the way economists work. Particular market changes may seem random and unpredictable, but sequences of changes often match uncannily – regardless of scale. Within huge reams of data lurks a bizarre order and symmetry, not of top and bottom or left and right, but of *scale*.

All this takes place at the level of statistical analysis. But in the actual day-to-day market, chaos is encountered in its more traditional sense, and this is the unpredictable modern marketplace described by Tom Peters in his book *Thriving On Chaos*. Changes in new technology, in patterns of consumption, globalisation of markets, currency fluctuations and business stability demand a sharp reassessment of old organisational priorities. Brave new companies must therefore adopt a devolved, flexible and amorphous style of management, and Peters puts the question: how exactly can companies survive the permanent, accelerating revolution that is today's business world?

His answer: embrace the chaos and turn it into a source of strength and market advantage. This entails:

- decentralising control systems (including the accounts systems managers who oversee them)

- decentralising strategic planning

- sharing information as widely as possible, at all levels

- training staff to understand this newly-available information, at all levels.

But the changes go further. Peters recommends, for instance, that most if not all organisational tools and resources be shifted to promote and support front-line action-taking and problem-solving – *immediately*. The decentralisation of strategic planning makes way for a radical new form of planning that is front-line driven and 'bottom-up', taking its cue from customers and suppliers. Above all, analysing the market to predict what it will do next is out; building skills and capabilities to take flexible action 'close to the market' is in.

In this scenario the chaotic marketplace is a reality, not an intuition of the future. The Peters account of daily and obligatory risk-taking in a mad world is apocalyptic and curiously out of control, as though he has taken on the characteristics of the chaotic phenomena he describes. His writing style is accordingly gung-ho, frantic, 'brainstormed', and immediate. If he pauses (the reader feels) the marketplace will change again, and his last point will be made redundant.

It is no doubt true that market forces are less regulated now than at any time in recent history, and that the unstable acceleration of such forces creates enormous upheaval for business. Peters' account of the 'madness' that is currently afoot makes heady reading. But his solution – to love the 'cataclysmic' conditions and 'cherish impermanence' – is self-consciously delivered in haste, so that it wilfully ignores any possibility of arriving at less 'mad' conditions. A moment's reflection would surely suggest alternative solutions – for example actions taken by elected representatives (governments) or their electors (citizens). This aspect of the 'chaotic' equation is barely mentioned. It seems a significant omission.

Peters' diagnosis presents a given reality ('market chaos') whose terms cannot be changed, regulated or re-organised, but must simply be suffered. Sensible forms of intervention for greater stability are never even considered, and companies (and their employees) are advised to accept an order that will consign most of them – as Peters convincingly details – to oblivion. But what would be the object of accepting such a scenario? And whose interests would it serve? Instead of attempting to thrive on 'chaos' (and to hell with the damned) wouldn't a saner project be to fashion from it some acceptable order?

Whatever the case, the decentralising and information-sharing trend urged by this species of guru has gained wide acceptance in company strategies; and downsizing, flat organisations and re-engineering could also be seen as strategies commended by Peters' work. Progressive companies are now seen as those which 'empower' their employees to deal with the information onslaught, and which remain flexible enough to react to – and welcome – the furious pace of market change. Other strategies like co-branding are different responses to this environment, as are all forms of 'listening' (including ongoing market research).

Downsizing, flat organisations, delayering, re-engineering

Phew – there's nothing like faddish language to make you feel disenfranchised. But all these weird compound verbs, re- and de-coinages are not really as difficult as they sound. They're poor pretenders, frightened of being unmasked and revealed for the dodgy metaphors and awkward euphemisms that they are.

'Downsizing' and 'delayering' both stem from a period of retrenchment and (as the tabloids described it) 'belt-tightening', in which efficiency was synonymous with being *lean* and *streamlined*. The strategic answer was to cut out the dead wood – those strata of (mostly) middle management seen collectively as an overhead that did not justify its cost. The organisational tail, it was thought, should not be allowed to wag the dog, so the 'lean' company externalised its work. It used outside consultants on an ad-hoc basis, rather than paying permanent in-house staff.

The word went out that organisations had too many people in them. And everyone believed it – whether it made sense or not. Nobody seemed to challenge the idea, although in many cases it was true. But the point is that the organisations should have been looking at this anyway – not waiting until a politician started a trend towards sacking people and pretending it was good for production. The basic half-truth here is about productivity.

Productivity is (as a raw measure) what you make divided by how many people make it. Twenty items made by ten people is apparently half as efficient as twenty made by five. So productivity rises if you sack people. It's as simple as that – in the short term. But what if the five can't get in more orders, or drag in the poor debts, or plan for the future? What if the cuts in staffing take you into the bone, let alone the flesh.

What happened in the 1970s and 1980s can be demonstrated by taking a broad view of one specific area of management – human resource management. In these days a manager applying for a job in HRM needed to have a strong awareness of redundancy law, procedures and implementation. Nobody in personnel could survive unless they could sack people efficiently and with no come-back. A generation grew up in HRM who were damned good at it – sacking, that is. But anyone who knows about HRM understands that best practice starts with a search for alternatives.

The most basic alternative to losing staff is to increase demand – to go out and get more orders or to create new markets. Instead, the people who could do that were 'let go', so we had a whole raft of people who were excellent at negative management and knew nothing about fostering growth or encouraging development. The option of losing all that expertise, skill, loyalty and knowledge, while at the same time building up a name as a hire and fire outfit is not the first one to pursue. When the upturn comes, how is the organisation seen? Where are all these people who knew how the business ran? Who wins?

'Delayering' was part of a move towards 'flatter' organisations, namely those seeking to avoid the old hierarchies in order to enable more efficient flows of information. In theory delayering need not demand large-scale redundancy programmes, but in practice they often happened as part of the restructuring and the apparent drive towards cost-efficiency.

What was the cost of this crazed pursuit of 'efficiency'?

The large-scale machinations, prompted in part by recession and falling profits, in part by a 'small is beautiful' management fad, caused untold misery in the labour market as mass sackings occurred and a prevailing redundancy atmosphere forced even good employees to move on. The cost of resorting to external consultants itself began to exceed expectations, a factor which seriously undermined the downsizing argument. Meanwhile older staff, with experience and loyalty born of many years' service, were summarily discarded in favour of younger recruits, creating curiously unbalanced companies of juvenile greenhorns working alongside a handful of guilt-ridden 'survivors'. (Some of the veterans, incidentally, would later be bought back again – at a higher price).

In short, the changes were destructive and demoralising for all concerned. Middle managers were not as much of a strategic liability as had been believed; in practice, they played a binding role in the organisation, mediating between the different levels of the hierarchy and relieving more senior managers of essential work which they were too busy to tackle. After downsizing, senior managers would often find themselves overwhelmed with administration. But a more fundamental problem also loomed: where would good senior management come from in the future, if not from good middle managers?

Ultimately, the insidious effect of widespread redundancy programmes made its mark on *all* employees – on families, friends and colleagues – and not just on those who had suffered directly. The new reality of insecure jobs and the so-called 'flexible' labour market decisively undermined the bond of loyalty that had long existed between employees and companies, devaluing the quality of countless working relationships.

The costly implications of the downsizing fad persist today, and are probably incalculable.

The paperless office

As we now know, the advent of computers heralded staggering possibilities and opportunities for businesses. Some of these opportunities were inevitably faddish, and the 'paperless office' was one such squib. The idea excited the virtual community's imagination by proposing that paper would become a thing of the past, finally rendered unnecessary by the *virtual office* – a cyberspace version of the one with handles.

In the virtual office, storage space for old-fashioned paper materials would no longer be needed. Vast volumes of information would be stored on hard disc, safely hibernating inside microchip circuitry. Computers could file information much more precisely and quickly than human beings, who usually had to heave open a filing cabinet full of dog-eared folders. Words and other information would only need to be teleported to 'our' world when we actually chose to print it out. Otherwise – no more filing cabinets!

The trouble was that microchips, for all their hyper-this and virtual-that, had a tendency to crash. Hair was torn out in clumps as managers lost incalculable amounts of information and labour-hours, then turned to their insurers for unlikely sums of money.

Computers came in between indexing systems (formerly based on the straightforward principle of shoving bits of paper into a drawer) and their innocent users. *Information processing* training now became as essential as coffee-breaks; people who had easily understood the user-friendly card indexing system now had to come to terms with non-intuitive software systems – and the relevant provisions of the Data Protection Act (which did not apply to paper indexing). The great leap forward, for some wretched antediluvians, ended in a Kafkaesque maze framed with light grey plastic.

The paper habit died hard. Like a flawed old friend, it was better trusted by the majority of people. Even the new computer technology seemed to share the human love of paper: computers *increased* rather than reduced paper usage, with more hard-copy documents being churned out than ever before. Suddenly it was possible to digitally process huge amounts of text, then tell your mouse to tell your pentium chip to tell your printer to run off nine or ten, or why not eleven – hundred? – copies of a document.

That's exactly what PC users did, which explains why the paperless office remains in every sense a virtual office, and an actual fad.

Consultation

Now here's a practice which divides fadologists. Some believed in it passionately, once upon a time, but their faith has foundered on disappointing experiences. Others practise it, but circumspectly, and without too much optimism. What follows is an account of consultation in action.

A large urban housing organisation with a sizeable government budget was given the task of regenerating not only a particularly depressed estate of high-rise council flats, but the local economic prospects of the residents as well. An entire social package was envisaged.

At the heart of the scheme was the principle of 'consultation', that is, of asking customers what they want. The residents knew what it was to have 'new plans' shoved down their throats – after all, their vandalised, dilapidated, dangerous tower blocks were themselves 'new plans' in the 1960s. The challenge now was, not to tell them what comes next on the menu, but to offer them some viable options and allow management decision-making to be guided by their response.

Tenant participation groups were established. Leaflets were distributed to notify public meetings and important community events. Residents were invited not only to help produce the estate's newsletter but also, if possible, to submit articles for it. At every level an attempt was made to involve them, and in particular, to integrate their preferences into big decisions.

The project has been a qualified success.

One serious problem was the attempt to introduce democratic debate into a community which had never experienced the luxury. Residents had come to believe that there was no point in trying to change anything, and dismissed all do-gooders (rightly, from experience) as establishment stooges. This kind of suspicion and apathy had led to a makeshift hierarchy of self-appointed 'community leaders' who had arrogated to themselves power – without a mandate. The law of the pack prevailed, with predictable consequences. There was no culture of participation in which different points of view could be aired. Abuse and intimidation dominated meetings.

So when consultative or democratic structures were introduced, there was a clumsy transitional period in which every level of decision, no matter how minor, had the magic wand 'consultation' waved at it.

Numerous evening meetings were now held on the estate – for *consultative* reasons. The employees of the housing organisation were obliged to attend them, often in a climate of mistrust and aggression. Even though these workers were giving up their evenings, anger was directed at them because they were the personification of past betrayal – and their encouraging statistics for 'local people employed' were announced to hoots of drunken derision and cynicism. But it's important to set this behaviour in context: no other channel of dissent had ever been made available to the residents.

Now here they all are, assembled to discuss the minutiae of their new houses and flats! What kind of doorhandles would the residents prefer? Where exactly in the kitchen do they want the cupboard units to go? What colour do they want the bathroom walls? And finally, when the architect asks, 'Would you rather have dormer or bay windows?', the tenants say, 'Don't ask us! You're the bloody expert – *you* design it'.

On the other hand, when a professional consultant strongly commends to the tenants a new computer-based repair notification system – which would almost certainly improve the quality of their day-to-day life – they reject it out of hand as an overpriced new-fangled gimmick. They opt instead for the older, less effective system.

This illustrates the thin line that consultation must tread, running the gauntlet between, on the one hand, properly eliciting people's wishes, and on the other, not wasting their time with trivia. It also implies (as in the example of the repair system) allowing people to choose options that the 'experts' might deplore. But that is the nature of freedom, and here the important point is not *what is chosen*, but the *opportunity to choose* – a right most people exercise (it's worth stating) without having to justify it. Many doctors, after all, smoke cigarettes.

Consultation means listening to people and offering them a choice – but a choice at a meaningful level. In housing, for instance, people are unlikely to want to choose every last detail of their light fittings; but they might want to veto the idea of dark alleyways running alongside their house.

When consultation is taken too far, it simply turns people off the principle. It certainly has its pitfalls, as outlined above.

Fadologists weighing the pros and cons need to ask the question: 'Is all the hassle of consultation worth it – and are the results better than those achievable with other methods?' (Clue: 'better' is the key word, and your answer depends on the objectives you want to prioritise).

ISO

How can you be sure of producing the same product, to the same quality, time after time – consistently?

Here's how. Watch the way the product is made, then take the formula and bottle it. Write a series of procedures which, when repeated faithfully, will produce the same result within very tight parameters. And there you are – standard procedure, standard product.

What can go wrong with this elementary principle? Well, the process objective is *consistent quality*. But if you set up a strict standard for a procedure which produces a poor result (i.e. a flawed product), then all you've done is guarantee the production of an immaculately consistent… flawed product. All the same standard of flaws.

Standards are essential, but it's important to keep your eye on the ball. The fact that there is a standard assures the system or the product, rather than the quality.

British Standard 5750 has been superseded by ISO 9000 (though as late as April 1997 some government departments were still using it as a minimum selection criterion for shortlisting contractors). One manager describes a college which proudly carried the BS

5750 kitemark on its letterhead – but when he asked a college worker about it, he was told: 'Yes, we do have the Standard in place here, but the system only applies to the way we run the car park.'

This wry response highlights a problem inherent in the Standard: how can an organisation lay claim to a standard when the system doesn't apply to the whole organisation?

CCT

Compulsory Competitive Tendering (CCT) arose from a government edict designed to:

- provide equal opportunities for service-providers to tender for work

- encourage competition, as an end in itself.

This was a political move to pressurise organisations into making certain kinds of choices under certain kinds of specified constraints. Its justification was the promotion of so-called 'free market' competition (though the word *compulsory* hardly sits comfortably with the language of laissez-faire economics). The law was framed as an attempt to disrupt the cosy relationship between, say, councils and favoured contractors, who would always end up getting certain jobs. Now the service-buyer would not only be obliged to put the job out to tender, but would also have to adopt prescribed selection criteria – once certain minimum standards had been met, the lowest bidder *had* to be awarded the contract.

The fad was imposed on a sometimes reluctant market. Though aimed at cutting costs, quality was harder to guarantee in advance now that service-providers were likely to be unknown to the purchaser. Where some long-standing arrangement existed with (for example) local office cleaners – who knew the job and did it competently with a level of commitment and loyalty – these could now be undercut by cheaper contractors. Whether the latter had any personal involvement in the work, any loyalty to the buyer, or even any interest in doing a good job, was impossible to determine in advance.

The fad raised the following question: is *cheapness* in itself more desirable than *value for money?*

Fiddling
with people

5

And the final batch of fads – people fads.

360° reviews

'Instead of the boss just appraising the performance of employees, why not also the other way around?'

So thought the 360° Review movement. This egalitarian-sounding exercise was meant to set working relations on a more reciprocal footing, so that control and guidance could come from different quarters within an organisation and not only from the 'top'. Unfortunately, it proved a recipe for discomfort and confrontation: bosses felt defensive and emasculated and employees resented their company insisting that they disclose their feelings.

Outward-bound activities/residentials

You want to know what your colleagues are really like – not in the office, but drifting together on a home-made raft towards a waterfall? You want to know the meaning of trust? You think your team works efficiently together? To find the answers, to get down to the nitty-gritty, you'd probably need to go on an *outward-bound* course.

These courses aimed at putting people through their paces, mentally and physically, so that they were forced to meet an exceptional challenge and discover resources that would then feed back into their team. Hazardous situations gave the activities an edge – 'you only find out who you really are when the chips are down', suggested the outward-bound philosophy – but they were (supposedly) comparable to daily teamworking situations.

In other words, your daily work performance was analogous to how well you, as individual or team, could skin a rabbit, build a shelter out of poo and garrotte a competitor from behind with a length of allotment netting.

This was the archetypal fad in its capacity to take a handful of exceptionally bland truisms (eg 'trust is important') and exaggerate it into an entire movement. As a result, flabby middle-aged managers would suddenly find themselves chewing locusts and drinking their own piss in freezing Dartmoor forests, while being barked at by half-man/half-wolf SAS colonels fresh from a cull. They would have to construct bivouacs out of sapling fibres, navigate their way across icy rivers by the night sky and daub their soft jowls with war-paint. Endurance in the wild reflected grit and determination at work, so unless you had a diagnosed case of coronary thrombosis you were unlikely to be let off this nightmare. Likewise, your ability to make quick judgements – should you push your weaker colleague out of the raft and drown him now, or would he be useful later in trapping a snake for your food? These experiences, though unlikely to help with Wednesday's invoice-processing, were somehow held to improve personal morale as well as *esprit de corps.*

This team-driven fad was highly influential. Some outward-bound activities were better organised than others, and no doubt some participants learnt something about themselves, but many felt that the activities were no more than an excuse to bully people. The background atmosphere was macho; the exercises were based on an obsolete boy's-fantasy survival-of-the-fittest principle; and in some cases the 'challenges' were manifestly dangerous, too. But above all, from the point of view of the Professional Fadologist, the *value* of outward-bound activities was unproven. To this day, no research or evidence convincingly demonstrates that surviving ScaFell Pike in winter helps you run a more efficient Bracknell post-room in spring.

Mufti days

Mufti or 'dressing down' days allowed staff to dress casually – in other words, to dress in a way favoured by each employee. The practice was developed in America, and typically one day in each month was set aside on which employees were commanded to feel relaxed and non-hierarchical. Sometimes companies would set up cross-team meetings so that individuals could get a wider sense of the organisation's work without their conventional clothes demarcating them by rank.

Often, however, the clothes in which they were to feel relaxed were also chosen. One large American financial services company issued its staff with a special mufti day T-shirt, tastefully emblazoned with the slogan: JUST ****ING DO IT. Unfortunately this did not encapsulate every employee's philosophy in their own words, even those who had always *just done it*. Some of the older members of staff felt embarrassed and offended; some younger members, denied full punk regalia, felt as uncomfortable in a T-shirt as a suit.

A British high street bank tried the mufti approach too, for one day each week. Here a different problem emerged: managers lost their nerve (and their status?) in casual clothing, and gradually reverted to the security of regulation clothing on the mufti days. Their non-work gear, like the prescribed slogan T-shirts, felt uncomfortable to them at work.

Alienation turned out not to be the best leveller – and here's the mufti rub. Since 'dressing down' days are always an organisational directive, their aim of encouraging self-expression is inevitably flawed: a specified mufti day implies that, as a rule, days are *non-mufti,* which on the idea's own terms means unrelaxed, uncomfortable and unchosen.

Performance-related pay

'In every work, a reward added makes the pleasure twice as great'
Euripides, Rhesus (c 455-441 BC)

Euripides' assertion is perhaps best illustrated in our own century by Stakhanov, a between-the-wars Soviet worker who, for his unique industrial productivity, was permitted a brief moment of glory by Stalin. Stakhanov was depicted on Soviet Realist posters as the model patriotic superworker, an example to his comrades, his exceptional performance rewarded with public acclaim.

The more recent version of performance-related pay, in effect, replaces Stakhanovite 'glory' with hard cash. The straightforward idea is that, above and beyond a basic component, your earnings are related to what you produce. Those who produce more, more efficiently, more quickly, reap the benefits in the form of better remuneration. If you produce twice as much – as Euripides might say – the pleasure is twice as great.

This reductive account, however, ignores a thorny problem. In an age when information and service industries are replacing traditional forms of industrial productivity, 'performance', 'output' and 'personal productivity' are far harder to measure. Interpersonal skills, for example, so fundamental to any consideration of performance, are subtle and intangible assets. They defy objective measure (*pace* psychometric tests) if only because they require *appraisal* – which is itself an interpersonal skill.

A second problem with individual performance-related pay is the atmosphere of competition it breeds, which can intensify to the point of self-destruction, generating mistrust and resentment within teams whose success depends on loyal co-operation. And finally, is it the group or the individual that should be rewarded for excellent team performance?

The performance-related pay model is still used, and some managers claim it as the single most powerful incentive in their inventory. But it is a fad, and the tide is slowly turning to reveal alternative perceptions of achievement and performance. Rather than the short-term carrot which generates short-term individual motivation and requires no understanding of the individual's organisational context or wider ethical duties, companies are increasingly seeing performance in terms of collective achievement – 'I cannot contribute successfully without your successful contribution'. Likewise, many employees will testify that, beyond a certain basic level, personal satisfaction is simply not related to remuneration. Cultures firmly predicated on the opposite view tend to store up a range of problems familiar to psychotherapists.

Performance-related pay can still be a worthwhile ingredient in pay packages if criteria and achievable targets are mutually agreed by employer and employee. But it is worth asking whether that marginal percentage gain, that sometimes misguided incentive, really justifies all the heat it generates.

Downshifting

'There is no joy but calm.'
Tennyson, The Lotus-Eaters (1842)

Nothing to do with skirts, and not to be confused with downsizing – though if you work for a downsizer you might be forced to shift down.

Downshifting was the stuff of *The Good Life* TV sitcom. It's a wish commonly nurtured today, the idea that instead of the habitual rhythms of modern employment – the long hours in traffic jams and on trains, the wasteful congestion, the toxic pollution, the endless staring at drab office walls, the futile round of daily work chatter, the dreary 11am coffee-breaks with the same weary faces – instead of all these repetitive, angry, *crushing* vanities…

…you escape! You flee to a calm, homely nirvana, spending each day contemplating the beauty of nature and, perhaps, practising the art of aromatherapy massage that you have yearned for so long to indulge! You can think about the *thisness* of your own unique navel. You can learn to play the harp, feel the aching pathos in your heart and give birth to that essential being curled foetally in your soul and crying for deliverance all these years.

Remember to make your plan. You will need:

- a small, spartan flat

- white walls

- a spare room, for the massage table

- a shelf (pine, undressed) for the essential oils

- a small display cabinet for the homeopathic remedies

- crystals, Royal Jelly and Sheela-na-Gig
- a stereo (preferably clockwork) for ambient vibes
- a garden, with a bit of grass (just in case)
- a violin.

Not bad. But first there's the question of getting a mortgage with your new freelance work status. And money might also be a problem if you can't get enough massage clients (there's no longer any regular pay cheque coming in). And what if you sprain your wrist and can't do any massage at all – how would you cope financially during periods of sickness?

While you are at work you may relish the thought of refuge from those dreary colleagues. But should you need a lift, the social function of the workplace will no longer be available to draw you out of yourself on bad days – and nor will the structure (essential, for many people) that imposes a dynamic pattern on each day.

Downshifting is a challenging aim to realise, personally and otherwise, and congratulations are due to those who have achieved the transformation. But do remember the experience of many downshifters before you who have felt, with hindsight, that the grass was greener for the conventional workhorses on the other side of the fence.

MBAs

The Master of Business Administration qualification was launched in the USA and has now been extended to a two-year course of study. It can be followed as a distance learning course or by conventional on-site instruction. At one time, managers everywhere thought the

MBA an essential route to business success, and a glut of newly-qualified graduates appeared on the scene, clutching their certificates – having completed a grinding course that was, after all, a largely theoretical exercise.

The MBA is no longer held in quite the same regard. Managers are rightly sceptical of business qualifications, since management is primarily a practical activity, a question of pragmatic decisions, action and contacts rather than theoretical rigour.

But some also ask 'What did managers do before the days of MBAs? Would the successful types really have achieved more if they had studied their profession first?'

NVQs

Over the past five years or so National Vocational Qualifications have been introduced to supersede the many qualifications (RSAs, City & Guilds and so on) that exist in diverse fields. They cover a range of vocational skills – from secretarial skills to design and technology and management skills.

The concept of the Vocational Qualification is a developmental one which stresses improvement in work performance. It is not just a question of acquiring skills (or 'competencies' in NVQ-speak) to get an initial foot in the door but, once employed, individuals can continue to improve their performance up to advanced levels.

The NVQ developed through functional analysis and provides credits for people as and when appropriate, in or out of work, relating to their skills and to work tasks they are able to perform. So an elementary level NVQ on 'Information Processing' might include basic office skills like answering a telephone call or using a filing system.

For managers, the set of standards is the MCI. Managers who want accreditation for these skills simply audit them accordingly and then seek the appropriate credit. However, some commentators have pointed to a discrepancy between the rhetoric of the NVQs and the reality – that instead of learning, managers just spend their time documenting what they do, then crafting it to the requirements of the standard. Having done this they can legitimately claim their accreditation of prior learning. But does the process actually teach them anything new about management?

Three-letter acronyms

The Three-letter acronym (TLA) fad is endemic amongst managers and their gurus. It's an unconscious fad, more like a nervous tic. Those who fall prey to this foible are almost always being either defensive, exclusive… or stupid.

One way of identifying TLA in action is to eavesdrop on managers' conversations. Listen out for sentences that have no intelligible nouns at all. What you might hear is something like the following:

'The TEC/LEC NVQ is based on TQM, but the GCSE is more IIP with a bit of QFD OK? It'll be a TPN on the QT!'

The best way of dealing with this is to wear one of those JVC headsets with built-in EQ FX. Tune in to REM on FM PDQ .

Investors In People

This was an idea that grew into an organisation… and a fad. It was an attempt to set up standards so that organisations would have defined objectives for professional personnel development. 'Do you tell people what their jobs are?' 'Is there a process for training?' 'What system of appraisal do you use?' are the kinds of question the IIP fad would focus on. Aficionados (and bystanders) would have an 'Investors' badge pinned on their chest to show they shared the values of the movement.

One training manager (anonymously) recalls going into a well-known high street chemist and finding the IIP certificate displayed proudly on the wall. Here was the incontrovertible evidence that this organisation's *people* had received extensive *investment* and knew just what they were about in terms of front-line customer care.

'So what's this all about, then?' the manager said to the checkout woman.

'Who knows', said the employee. 'You'll have to ask the boss.'

The badge or the journey

There are some central and common points about Investors in People that underpin a lot of what we're saying about fads.

First, seeing people as a resource worth investing in was a good idea before the Investors in People label was ever added to it, before it became a formalised process and certainly before it was privatised. The concept is that a good organisation tells its staff what it is doing and then clarifies with the people what their role is in working towards organisational success. Now they know what they are there to achieve, their training needs are identified and the appropriate development activities are provided. The success of these is monitored and is used to help plan the future arrangements.

It's not hard to grasp, really, and any good organisation would say this is common sense whether it's got a badge on it or not.

But it's the badge that causes a problem. Is the purpose to get the badge or to implement good practice? The two things are not necessarily the same and can be mutually exclusive, although those running programmes like IIP will clearly maintain that they demand high professional standards from their consultants and assessors. But if a company needs IIP (like it might need ISO 9002) to be considered for a contract, what is the driving force? Is it to develop a sound human resource system in the company, or to bash through the essential steps and do just enough to get the badge (even if it does mean trying to blur a few edges along the way?)

Don't get us wrong. IIP people are very ethical and highly trained. But there is always scope for someone to try and rip off the system if the rewards come from getting a piece of paper rather than really espousing good business practice. But then again, there would be fewer organisations that even thought about the value of their people as a resource, unless there were some sort of tangible reward, so perhaps the purist view has to be tinged with a fair shade of reality.

TQM

TQM swept the board as the dominant fad of the early 'nineties. TQM stands for total quality management. It took the prevalent fascination about quality and expanded it to encompass a range of different management ideas. However, at heart TQM was and is simple. In many ways TQM fitted the political ideology of the kind. In TQM, the customer is king, but everyone has a role.

To understand TQM there are a number of simple ideas to get to grips with.

One, quality is measured against what the customer requires – in terms of performance, timing and cost. Quality is either right or wrong, it is not a question of relative worth. This is where fitness for purpose comes into the equation and it has nothing to do with what the organisation thinks it wants to offer or what staff want to give to suit their convenience.

Two, everything the supplier does needs to be aimed at providing a quality service. And suppliers are not only those people who meet the end user. Inside the organisation there are chains of customers and suppliers who all have to receive the right quality for the process to be completed properly.

Three, we find out what customers want by asking them (including our internal customers – our colleagues inside the organisation to whom we provide goods, services or information) and then we gear the service around that.

Four, bad quality costs money.

Five, in the process, everyone needs to be involved in looking for ways to continually improve what is on offer. This means people need to be empowered to come up with ideas and do them. In the end, the total quality of the business will improve.

Six, teams are the best way of delivering a quality service which may mean removing the traditional demarcation between jobs.

Sounds too good to be true? Well in many cases it was. So what went wrong with TQM? Well, often the initiatives got stuck in the organisational mud. Many of the improvements were intangible and the bottom liners started to get nervous. Teamwork is fine, as is empowerment, but it ruffles feathers, especially amongst the 'haves'. And then there was the evangelising. TQM came with baggage – if you weren't part of a caring sharing quality circle then you were in trouble.

But the biggest problem, the greatest barrier, was a lack of top-down commitment. Senior management said that quality really mattered, that teams ruled, that ideas for improvement had to flow and be listened to… and then proceeded to make it clear that none of this applied to them. It was all right for the lower orders, but those at the top did not really feel that they had a responsibility to deliver the promises they had made to subordinates, or to take responsibility for the quality of their own work or decisions. And so it caved in.

This is perhaps the greatest issue around fads – lack of top management commitment and role modelling. We'll return to it a little later.

Stop the world...

...or how to lose the bathwater and keep the baby

6

So far we've listed and looked at several management fads and a few gurus. But the trouble is that the whole world of fads is spinning so fast that if you wanted to take a photograph of it, it would always be blurred. Things change and evolve at such a rate that by the time you see the picture clearly, it has changed. It's like the Tom Peters issue we raised earlier – pause and the market place moves on.

So what we are going to do is to freeze the whole scene. We want to stop the frenetic and frantic chase for fads and look inside them, underneath them and through them. We want to see what really makes them tick, look at whether there are good sides to them and explore the role of consultants. But first we need to look at what makes the managers tick – the ones who buy the fads and the ones who don't.

Why some managers love fads

Let's start with a positive view of the managers who are working with a fad for the right reasons.

Some magnificent managers are working now, to introduce a fad to an organisation. They may be fairly new to the business and have identified that a radical change in culture or operations is needed. They are using a fad as a Trojan Horse, to change the way the organisation works or to undermine an inappropriate culture that hasn't shifted much in decades. Or they could be aiming to focus attention on a fad and under the guise of a single initiative to raise and tackle a long agenda of linked issues. Or it could be a way of getting to those managers in the few dark corners of the organisation that still haven't quite reached the second half of the twentieth century, without launching a frontal attack on them.

But these are perhaps in the minority. The other strand of management – those who do it because it sounds like a good wheeze – is at best wasting the organisation's time and money, and at worst helping to reduce morale, motivation and performance.

The uncommitted top manager

There is one especially dangerous managerial type who loves fads. It's the top manager who spots something in the management journals or is told about a superb experience that a colleague in another organisation is having with this particular firm of experts. 'Not cheap, but worth every last EMU'. The belief is that someone else can come in from outside and 'do something' to the organisation that will make it much better. And if a multi-national somewhere is doing it, it must be good so they want to be seen to be at the cutting edge. These are the people who would buy our JR spoof.

The consultants are brought in and given the job of taking the organisation forward… without top managers having to do anything active themselves. The TQM programme (or whatever) is launched and then starts halfway up the organisation. A working party / implementation taskforce / steering group or project team is formed to run it… 'on behalf of the management team'. The bullshit is that it helps the development and corporate strategic future of those on the project team… that the real push is coming from top managers and the middle people on the project team are only doing the detailed implementation bit… and so on.

But the process never touches the senior managers and the consultants never see them again. The Head of Human Resources is given the lead role (again) because it's a people issue (what isn't?). Lower echelons notice the absence of top managers and mutter that they've been here before with earlier fads… and that if it isn't good enough for the boss, it isn't good enough for them… and if they can't be bothered, I'm damned if I'm going to take it seriously!

Inexorably, the fad grows an extra 'e' and starts to fade. The consultants breathe a few gasps of life into the sinking body, but it is doomed. The lack of commitment or role modelling from the top means no action further down and not a snowball's chance of the fad taking root.

Believe it – it is as simple and clear-cut as that. The trouble is that many of these particular top people never monitor whether the techniques became embedded and started to work in the first place – let alone produced a worthwhile pay-off. So they're suckers for the next fad to come along.

The magic wand brigade

Further down the organisation are managers who see fads as an instant solution, an off-the-shelf quick fix and a magic wand.

It's a misguided and naive approach, full of good intentions but ill thought out and fundamentally flawed.

A parallel is the classic quote about motherhood and apple pie. Ask a sample of people if these are good things and you get a positive response from 99%. Most automatically accept the rightness of it and few of the others dare (or can be bothered) to argue, even if they do have an opinion.

It is often like this when you look at fads. A successful fad is one where it begins to make sense as soon as you start to examine its key components. It should be simple (even simplistic) and popular. Anyone should be able to understand what it is about and it should be as unchangeable as motherhood. In other words, wrap it up so that it raises quality levels, increases motivation or makes people better at their jobs and it must be a good idea. Nobody would say any different.

So a successful fad has to be obvious. The outline must be so clearly worth investigating and impossible (or very difficult) to resist. And you have to be able to unpack it's components so that every manager can relate to it, while at the same time there has to be just enough of an element of professional expertise and mysticism to give the management consultants something to live off. For a fad to be successful it must be initially transparent to all and then become blurred, needing experts' eyes to help you focused on its detail.

Depending on who you are – and how prepared you are to stand up and say that this is more transparent than mystical – you find some self-evident truths sitting there when you start to analyse some top fads.

There comes a point when you suspect that either you have missed the point, or this fad is simple and straightforward common-sense. If that's the case, why do we need a guru to tell us this? Why aren't we doing this anyway?

The problem is, of course, that if all the other organisations and managers are singing the praises of this fad, it is very threatening and risky indeed to stand out against it and criticise. Far easier to nod knowingly, say the right things and keep your head down.

We would argue that there is a direct relationship here, with the confidence that managers have in their own expertise and their level of knowledge about management, as an activity in its own right. It is a statement we can make only as a deduction from experience, but we believe that many managers just don't live up to their job titles. They do as much lower-level work as they can themselves, rather than manage and co-ordinate the other people doing the work, whom they are meant to be leading.

Don't get us wrong, though. This situation – while relatively widespread in our experience – is by no means always the fault of the individual. The organisation has let them down by giving them the job without giving them the right tools to do it. Many people in charge of large workforces and serious levels of physical resources have had – and still get – little or no management training from their employers. All the evidence shows this to be especially true for those in middle management, where they struggle on and do their very best… and they often do it pretty damn well! But promotion has come not for their potential in leading others in this management role, but as a reward for being good at the last job. And the last job was, by definition, less managerial, more technically or task based and hands-on.

Such managers have to invent their own definition of their management role and it often is that they are there to do the same work as the rest of their team, or to solve their team's problems when they get it wrong. Nobody has ever told them any different.

Focusing on these activities means they have no time to plan ahead and identify and remove potential problems and difficulties. They fight fires instead of looking at fire prevention. They're very, very busy sorting out problems that shouldn't have happened… and there just aren't enough hours in the day to look ahead.

Then you can add to this the entirely understandable human attitude, that many of them like their last job better than this one and they don't really want to stop doing what they did before. They are not motivated to let go of the old role and adopt the new one, so they fail ever to do so.

Untrained melody

At this point we considered adding the process of management development to our list of fads. In some quarters it is this month's top tune, or seen as a wheeze that is over and above the basics of running a business. It isn't! There is no sensible alternative to managers learning what the job of management is about, in the same way as an accountant needs to learn about financial reports, accounting procedures and the legal constraints of company law.

For the simple reason that management development is so central to business success, we struck it off the list of fads.

Managers do not acquire all the skills, insight, knowledge or understanding to co-ordinate large budgets, big teams of people and massive sets of physical resources, by magic. It isn't something you just 'do'. It can be argued that a huge chunk of management is simply common-sense, made mystical by those who make their living by running training courses. And there may be a germ of truth here somewhere, for some training providers. But excellent management development does a great deal more than offer quick-fix techniques, or a set or instructions that everyone can follow, to get it right.

It should provoke questioning and thought, raise doubts and propose the odd heresy. It must make managers think, reflect, review and consider what effect they have on their colleagues, customers, staff and processes.

Fad-free zones

Having touched on senior managers who do not own the process of implementing a new management technique, and those who see it as a panacea, we can look at a diametrically opposed set of individuals. These are the sophisticated, skilled, committed and truly effective managers. They are not necessarily the MBAs and in many cases they act as they do without any serious training. But they delegate, empower, communicate like mad down, up and across the organisation, and they care about people and results. And they simply don't bother with other people's fads. They dismiss the very idea of any universal formula that claims to solve a business problem in every unique organisation.

They know what their organisation is doing, how it works and what makes it tick. Their businesses approach is to adopt simple and sound business practice, and the crucial point is that they have been quietly doing what the fad advocates for ages. While their own version does not have the same catchy name as the current fad, they've been doing it here for years as they work to raise standards and performance quietly and with no fuss.

If they were to adopt a fad it would be because they have looked at the idea and its structure, seen it to more than a simple statement of good practice in any situation and decided that it will work for them. They will have asked whether there is more benefit than cost, what the implications are, how hard this is going to be and whether there's a potential return on investment. The model manager for fad-spotting, in our terms, is neither gullible to the point where they embrace any new fad with religious fervour, nor Luddite to the extent that they say it won't work here, before they have heard the story.

Let's try this out. We'll explain a couple of major fads and you can see just how innovatory they really are.

Investing in your people

Investors in People is a laudable and virtually unchangeable philosophy. You get a badge to show the outside world that you believe that your people are the major resource in the business. To get the award you must achieve the set standard, producing clear evidence and achieving success in a rigorous and criteria-based assessment which examines whether you have systems in place for:

1 Committing the whole organisation – from the top – to training and development as a core business activity, and explaining to individual employees that their own training is going to help them achieve success, once they know what their role is and how they contribute to the success of the business

2 Identifying the training and development needs of all employees (in consultation with them), by comparing the individual's current skills against the requirements of their specific job now and in the foreseeable future

3 Making arrangements to plug the gaps identified in training needs analysis, with courses, coaching, open learning, mentoring or whatever

4   Reviewing the success of the training, in terms of how well what has been delivered really did support the achievement of the original goals and the organisation's business aims, objectives and long-term plans, as well as the immediate reactions to a good day out.

To get the award the organisation's employees are interviewed, sampled in surveys and observed. Examples of the paper systems are collated and put into files to demonstrate beyond doubt that this organisation does all these things. Only when it does does it merit the title, *Investor in People.*

Good stuff! But is it really revolutionary? Many managers will be asking how else can you run a business, so what is this really saying? Let's take it step by step and, as you read it, make a note of any issues that you think are not applicable to any sound business, whether an *Investor in People* or not.

1   If you want a great business, make sure you know where the business is going and where changes might take place. You need to look out for potential market shifts, mergers and acquisitions, changing customer requirements, new competition and developing technology and other factors that will impact on the organisation and its success.

2   Then tell everyone who works for and with you what their job is and what results you expect from them – explaining how the company may need to develop in the light of any changes you spotted in your analysis. Explain where their work, their part of the process fits into the overall whole. Make sure they understand exactly what they have to do, in order to make a success of it and say clearly that you believe in training and development as a way of helping them do their jobs well or better.

3 Next, get line managers and supervisors to talk to their people and compare their current and anticipated job roles with the range of skills they have now. Are they fully equipped to do everything required of them – or do they need training to run the new machines that are coming, or to sharpen customer care skills? If so, what are the specific areas where people need training?

4 Arrange the training, to suit the situation. So if 20 people need the same thing, run a course. If it's one, find a more targeted approach.

5 Find out whether it worked. See whether the investment paid off and attempt to measure the change in behaviour or performance that the employee is showing, after training. Then review the whole training policy, see if it worked and then plan next year's budget and targets.

Revolutionary, eh? That stuff about telling people what their role is and what is expected of them… that's powerful! And whether or not your organisation works like this, the chances are that you made very few, if any, notes.

Unfortunately, the reality is that in many organisations even these obviously important actions do not happen. There is far too little of some of the aspects outlined above – especially the ones about explaining why, or reviewing success. So before you scoff too much at the need to have a label for *Investors in People*, just think about how many mistakes are made in organisations, because someone assumed that such-and-such was what was needed. And the reason they assumed was that nobody told them!

The bottom line, though, is that the five stages outlined above make perfectly normal business sense to the vast majority of individuals. Shareholders certainly might want to ask whether there is any other way to run a business.

The reason that *Investors in People* is defensible as an initiative – even though it is sound, everyday business strategy badged up as a national standard, is because of the examples we mentioned earlier. In many cases it is a fad acting as a Trojan Horse, rolled into the company gates to develop a range of good practice where several large gaps existed before, or to get into the dusty corners of the organisation where little light shines. And there is nothing wrong with achieving national recognition for success, physically demonstrated in the badge and the title.

Our point, though, is that there is absolutely nothing new in it. It is obvious. Any decent book on human resource management written in the last couple of decades will spell all this out in words of one syllable – but without the label.

And this is the acid test. If the organisation principally wants *Investors in People* for the badge that comes at the end of the journey… it's a fad. But if the journey itself is more important than the award, then it's probably being undertaken as a Trojan Horse, for some pretty sound reasons.

Managing quality

Total quality management (TQM) is based on some sound principles. It uses teams, communication, analysis, review and problem-solving to bring performance nearer the required standard, consistently.

Customers dictate the specification and the organisation gears up to deliver what the customer wants, every time.

The essential starting point is a switch from the production-driven philosophy to a customer-facing approach. It is a shift from, 'how can we sell to the market what we're good at making and like doing', to, 'what does the market need and how can we meet that need'?

The fact that it became a fad in the 1980s is a great shame, because the underlying principles are about reducing waste by up to 40%, enhancing communication and problem-solving at all levels of the workforce, raising motivation and building cross-functional teams.

As a serious management approach it is powerful, difficult, empowering and uncomfortable for most traditional managers. To become effective and a real part of the organisation's culture it has to be owned by the people who work there. This raises another issue of faddism and the role of consultants.

Two types of consultant

There is nothing wrong with the notion of consultants, (we would say that, wouldn't we, as that's what we do most of the time). But there are different forms of consultancy, each suited to a specific type of problem.

Expert consultants come in and put right something that has gone wrong. Then they leave, having mended it. So any sort of service engineer, software development consultancy, recruitment agency, training company or counselling service will tend to do the work for you, as a sub-contractor. They are doubtless very expert, but when they pull out the service stops operating.

Process consultants, on the other hand, are the ones who come in for most flak. These are the people who are accused of borrowing your watch so they can tell you the time. But they are entirely suited to an issue like TQM, where the organisation and its managers have to adopt and then nurture the processes for themselves, even when the consultants are long gone.

Not all the consultants who led the TQM boom in the 1980s were as skilled in the process themselves as they could or should have been. As TQM took off it looked as if there was an increasing need for more consultants to introduce it to organisations. There were not enough clued-up process consultants around to do all the work, so some consultants started to market a TQM service that was less than 100% solid. In particular, there was a need to be hard and strong, about the vital importance of the company owning the process and the commitment, and leading from the top by example and clear commitment.

Obviously, we can't explain all there is to know about TQM in a couple of pages, but we'll try and give you the essentials.

TQM shifts the emphasis from finding errors after they've been made, to preventing them happening. It removes or reduces the expert role of the white-coated quality manager who stands at the end of the process and weeds out the faulty goods and services, and gets every individual along the way to accept that she or he is responsible for their own quality.

A traditional target of, say, 5% error is the same as saying you want it done 95% right. This leads to a culture where less than perfect is acceptable. With TQM the aim is to get it right first time, every time, to the required standard that the customer requires. (What the customer requires is the only specification – what you can do is irrelevant, if it doesn't match).

Instead of seeing other functions within the organisation as the enemy, TQM says that each is an internal customer of another part or parts of the company and an internal supplier to others. So in a production setting you receive part-finished goods from an internal supplier, which is the process that comes before yours. You are therefore their customer. If what they supply you with is sub-standard there is nothing you can do and they have let their customer down. The same principles apply when you pass it down the line to your internal customer or customers.

Within these chains of suppliers and customers, people at every level work as teams, talk to each other and try to solve problems. It is a less hierarchical arrangement than usual and people across the organisation are empowered to review any mistakes, work out why they happened and plan steps to manage them out of the process. Each time this happens the result is that the products are nearer the specification standard – less deviation and a lot less wasted time, material and energy.

There's a lot more to it than that, but that's it in a nutshell.

TQM is not a quick fix

The point that emerges from this very scant overview of TQM is that it involves fairly massive changes to issues as major as organisation culture, communications, levels of authority and inter-departmental/functional relationships. There is a new vision of quality and customers needed, which takes energy and effort, to win the hearts and minds of all the staff. There are new skills to be learnt, in problem solving, measuring and analysing results, planning continuous improvements, and so on and so on.

Therefore, a firm of expert consultants coming in for three months to implement TQM has virtually no chance of success. It is a marathon, not a sprint and the only approach that works is for process consultancy to start top down, and to instil the values and install the techniques among the key senior people. Then it can cascade down the organisation and is owned from within.

But how many people have experienced a failed TQM project, where it was limited to a time scale and a budget that meant it never could work, and/or where it was started not at the top, but halfway down, leading to the disaffection we have pointed to on more than one occasion already.

TQM, handled properly, is an excellent and powerful approach. Some argue that it is the only game in town, and it is hard to defeat their case. TQM is a culture change that aims for continuous improvement which, by definition, is a never-ending journey. It needs people to start seeing the world from a whole new vantage point – with the customer slap bang in the middle, and other colleagues as that customer, in many cases. It requires a shift in thinking, from 'what can we make' to 'what do they need' and it shares some attributes with Just in Time techniques. It breathes the air of openness, communication, teams and is an organisation that learns from its mistakes. It depends on targeted training to meet identified needs, a programme of team briefing or other forms of awareness raising, delegation, empowerment and joint problem-solving.

But TQM has failed in many organisations where it was introduced as a fad!

The lesson here is that, if it is sound business practice, take it seriously – allocate the time and the resources and make sure it is owned and led from the top with commitment and passion. Leave it to external consultants and advisers to do it to you and you will not make it. But more than that, the experience will come back to haunt you, as it turns people off the essential principles of quality management for years to come.

Common factors

One final point in this chapter. Did you notice that in the paragraph above that starts 'TQM, handled properly…' there are some other fad names cropping up? Empowerment… learning organisations… Just in Time… training (à la *Investors in People*), teamworking and so on?

If you work for a company that seriously operates TQM, it is odds on that you operate in a culture where it is normal to communicate well and to trust and train people. It will be second nature to develop and use teams where appropriate, pass as much authority down the line as is realistic and practical, and to value learning so that experiences are examined to identify where improvements could be made.

This is all round good practice and it is actually very hard to introduce any single fad, without having others in place. Most fads are a variation on the theme of sound management, but they chip off just one aspect of what should be a holistic approach. So if an organisation is already working effectively with TQM then it has almost certainly adopted most or all of the other approaches. Each one links into and depends on several others.

But we want to leave you with a strong and clear message. Don't blame the gurus for the fads. Certainly question whether any guru is worth following, because s/he cannot know your circumstances and their approach is possibly trans-Atlantic, out of date or theoretical. But if they are making sense in their guruesque writings, think through the whole issue.

The bottom line is… don't go for the soundbites and don't get fadded!

The last chapter of this book has a few details of some major gurus and their ideas. The points we make are brief and we don't claim to do them full justice – so read what they say, for themselves.

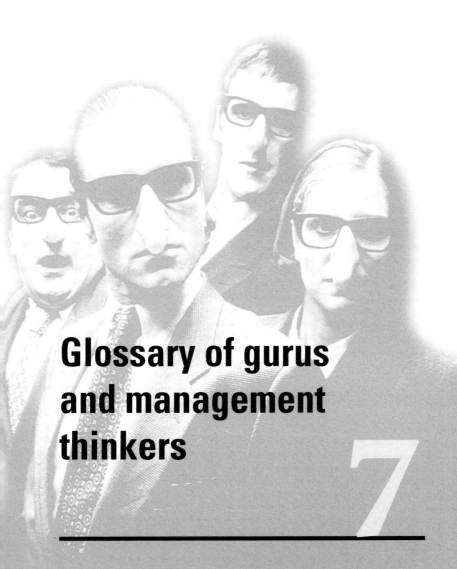

Glossary of gurus and management thinkers

This glossary consists of economists, philosophers, theorists and management gurus. Some are wise; some venerable; others more than venerable – dead. Many fall into the category of great management thinkers and are beyond reproach. But each would understand the phenomenon (and, no doubt, the absurdity) of the fad. And they would probably also explain, however, why their own particular theory or prescription is *not* actually a fad.

Please accept that what follows is a very potted version of these people's ideas. For the full monty read their own words.

Argyris, Chris

Argyris' work focused on middle management. He proposed that managers at this level unconsciously sabotaged the organisation's work through their defensive style. He painted a portrait of such managers as being fearful of risks, watching their own backs and not trusting their colleagues both above and below them in the organisational hierarchy.

He maintained that this defensiveness – the result of fear that the manager could lose their control over others – often stopped them going far enough down the road of letting individuals develop the full extent of their potential, which would operate for the good of both the individual and the organisation.

The later (stereotypical) perception of this managerial stratum as dispensable and even poisonous probably owed something to Argyris' brand of social psychology.

Belbin, R Meredith

Devised a process for categorising the team roles needed in a mature team, and analysing, through an inventory of questions, which roles individuals were strongest in. By reviewing what exists and how people's strengths match up, the roles can be examined and analysed to help form a balanced team.

In most cases, a manager would recognise not so much what Belbin has written, but the inventory which is used on many courses and team-building activities.

The basic notion is that a team needs to have a range of people in it, with various team roles. (Team roles are not necessarily the same as roles outside the team.) What is looked at is the mix of styles needed to build a coherent and balanced team. It needs, for instance, someone to manage the process, someone to trigger creative thinking, someone to do the basic detailed stuff… and so on. No role is more important than the others and all are needed.

Deming, WE (quality)

One of the founders of the quality movement and extremely highly rated in Japan. As a statistician, Deming's view is that quality is achieved by setting the right standards and then conforming to them. If there is a right way to do something, the quest for quality is about getting that result more consistently every time, via statistics and control mechanisms that aim to remove inconsistency.

Deming is quoted as maintaining that 85% of all product faults are the direct result of management and managers. In other words, get the management right if you want quality to be right, and don't try to start at the bottom.

Drucker, Peter

Perhaps the greatest influence on management thinking this century. He described privatisation in a book as long ago as 1969 (*The Age of Discontinuity*) and was perhaps the originator of management by objectives.

His influence is felt in the work of many successor 'gurus' and his comments were so wide-ranging that they can't all be summarised here. However, one area where he is recognised as a leader in the field was in defining what managers do, in five stages. They:

- set objectives and work out plans for getting there
- organise people and other resources to deliver the plans
- motivate, lead and communicate with people
- measure, analyse and interpret how well things are going
- develop themselves and others.

Hammer and Champy

Michael Hammer and James Champy are the pioneers of Business Reengineering (mentioned earlier), who maintain that companies must start to carry out a fundamental reinvention of everything they do.

Companies have to scrap all their ideas about what makes a well-structured and properly run organisation, and start with a clean sheet. The basic tenet is that Adam Smith (two centuries ago) said that the whole process of work breaks down naturally into smaller tasks and activities. Industry has worked on these lines since then, and it's time for a shake-up.

There has to be a move, they say, back to a unified view of work and examining how best today's businesses can be run, to deliver the right outcomes.

There also has to be a critical analysis of the rules and conventions by which companies are run. We get repairs done by contractors. *Why? Can't we do it? Does it need doing? Is it cheaper to scrap the machines and buy new ones?* Decisions on this are the prerogative of the accounts department. *Why? Is this right? Does it make sense? What are the alternatives and is one of them better?*

Handy, Charles

Long-time management guru in the UK, with several best-selling books to his name. He focuses on change and how organisations need to constantly monitor what is happening, and he predicted years ago that the flexible labour market – in some detail – was coming. Handy has devised various models of organisations to cope with changing needs and he also is a leading light in the field of organisation culture.

With Roger Harrison he devised perhaps the best known approach to assessing and understanding organisation culture, using the four strands of power, achievement, role and support (which he elsewhere describes by writing about four Gods of Management).

Herzberg, Frederick

A motivational guru who reasoned that what motivated people was not the same as what turned them off. People are motivated by challenge, responsibility, seeing the results of their work and so on.

They are turned off by being paid too little or having poor working environments (hygiene factors).

But, paradoxically, sorting out a hygiene factor simply means removing a source of discontent. It does not mean that it can act as a positive motivator. So if someone works in a cramped and stuffy office, they are demotivated until it is sorted out. But once they have enough space and ample ventilation, giving them even more does not then motivate them. That requires the issues that cluster around the title of 'job satisfaction'.

Money is not, therefore, a real long-term motivator, although unfairness in pay or a wage packet that is less than needed will demotivate and cause problems.

Juran, Joseph M

A contemporary of Deming who comes at quality from an entirely different angle. It is about top-down commitment, teams, communication and ownership at all levels in the organisation (backed up with appropriate systems). Responsibility for quality cannot be delegated or abdicated; everyone must take responsibility for their own quality.

In many ways, this is the bedrock of the TQM movement.

Likert, Rensis

Concentrated on the organisation's management style and maintained that a collaborative, involving and participative management style would get better results and more productivity from an organisation than would a directive and instructional approach.

McGregor, Douglas

McGregor was an American social psychologist who developed the concept of the 'X Manager' and the 'Y Manager'. These were archetypal characterisations of two opposing psychological approaches to management. The X Manager assumes that individuals are fundamentally lazy and ill-motivated and will only work if rewarded with appropriate incentives. The Y Manager, on the other hand, assumes that individuals want to do their job efficiently and will try their best, given the opportunity. In short, the formulation pits *authoritative* against *participative* styles of management.

Whether these interesting psychological profiles are of any help to real flesh-and-blood managers is a moot point. But readers of philosophy and politics will recognise in McGregor's characterisations the two classical views of human nature – the reactionary version found in Hobbes' *Leviathan,* and the liberal view in the work of William Godwin and Paine's *Rights of Man.*

Maslow, Abraham

Another leader in motivation theory, who drew up a hierarchy of needs. It says that people have basic needs (shelter, food etc) that must be met before any more sophisticated needs can become motivators. So if your family is hungry, you don't worry about recognition at work, you concentrate on bringing home food. But once you can do that, food no longer occupies your motivational mind and you start to look for satisfaction from other more sophisticated rewards. These move up the hierarchy and include social acceptance, recognition, responsibility and control of your own destiny.

Mayo, Elton

Work is a social activity and the most critical motivating factors are those which feed the psychological needs of the individual. Teams and groups at work are a prime force in developing organisational success and human relations are at the heart of what makes this success real.

Sometimes known as the human relations guru, he described his view that workers are governed by emotional reactions while managers react with logic and rationality – so unless some understanding and empathy takes place there will be conflict.

Moss Kanter, Rosabeth

A modern guru, professor and editor of the Harvard Business Review. Empower the people to improve the organisation. Make organisations in the 1990s leaner, fitter and less managed, so they can adapt and flex to suit the changing requirements of the fast-moving environment.

The thrust of much of Moss Kanter's work was that organisations should aim to do more with less.

Pareto, Vilfredo

We mentioned Pareto analysis earlier, but we have included some extra notes on Vilfredo because he is an example of a guru whose work is used and adapted all over the commercial and industrial world.

He was a noble Italian economist who, in 1897, worked out that there was a mathematically constant relationship in the spread of wealth in England. So 20% of the population has 80% of the income and this was replicated across other countries, when he looked into it. This principle has been developed into a range of versions, some very simple indeed. For example, on World Service radio in September 1997 a talk was given on the number of dental cavities that occur among people who live in areas where there is a high level of lead pollution. The actual statement was that 80% of the cavities occur in 20% of the sample – an exact illustration of the basic concept that people Pareto was putting forward.

His work was extended by a number of later gurus, such as George K Zipf, who postulated the 'Principle of Least Effort'. This says that 20% of the resources (human or otherwise) generally produce 80% of the output.

Then, Juran (qv) used the 80:20 rule to find quality flaws, on the basis that 80% of the problems come form 20% of the sources.

Even today Pareto's work is being extended. One of the recent books (by Richard Koch) that we mention at the very end of this chapter revisits his theories, reviews other earlier developments and adds a new dimension.

Peters, Tom

Wrote (with Robert Waterman) the best-selling management book of all time, *In Search of Excellence.* He also wrote *Thriving on Chaos* which was discussed earlier. He has said a great many things in his writings and his seminars; we touch on only a couple here.

Peters is quite heavily McGregor Theory Y, with a virtually diametrically opposed view to Taylor. He says that if you give people something worth doing, train them properly and then let them get on with it, they will perform superbly for you in virtually every case. People are creative, trustworthy, committed and intelligent, he says – while customers are rude, demanding, unrealistic and… customers.

It is restrictive management (and the need for written instructions that tell you when and how to take breaks, or go to the washroom) that causes people to act like they are dull, he says. Treat them that way and that's how they'll act – and when they do they act that way to customers.

His aim is to prompt managers to keep reinventing new and better ways of doing things, as the world is changing so fast that standing still is not an option.

Schonberger, Richard

Writer on operational management. Best known for *Japanese Manufacturing Techniques* (1982), which examined the 'Just-in-Time' or Toyota System of plant and scheduling management. The work followed in the wake of the '70s energy crisis and focused on consequential storage costs, which were minimised in Toyota manufacturing systems.

In *Building a Chain of Customers* he described the notion of a series of internal customers, all requiring good service from their internal suppliers if the end user was to get the right outcomes.

Taylor, Frederick

One of the very early management gurus who invented what is now seen as the outdated view of management as 'scientific'. It sees tasks as essentially practical, with people fitted in to do what is needed rather than tasks altered to suit peoples' capabilities, preferences or motivation. There is a strong hint of time and motion used to define how tasks should be done consistently.

Taylor was clear that a task had to be clearly specified or people would get it wrong. Even shovelling had to be set out as a series of steps, each with a time attached – not least because of the very strong hint that people who shovel are basically incapable of thinking it out for themselves.

You may want to look back at McGregor's Theory X, and remind yourself that Taylor was writing several decades ago!

Recent arrivals

The age of the guru is still with us and fads look unlikely to disappear just yet. As our parting shot we have just scanned the current month's books that have landed on our desks. We haven't read them yet so can neither recommend nor describe them. We sincerely hope they are about sound management approaches rather than fads and we know that there are inevitably some nuggets of common-sense in them.

Robert Cooper and Ayman Sawaf

A book called 'Executive EQ: Emotional Intelligence in Business'. The cover and the strapline to the book say it is about using self-motivation and knowledge of one's own emotions (and those of others), so as to control them and to thus master the workplace, increase profitability and compete for the future. It includes the world's first EQ map, tested on thousands of managers in hundreds of organisations.

Richard Koch

The book is 'The 80/20 principle: The secret of achieving more with less'. Interestingly, although we have not read the book, it is plain that Pareto's work on 80:20 has become accepted wisdom and has been developed by later gurus.

This makes Pareto a guru and not a faddist (plus of course, he is dead) and makes his work a sound concept for use by management. The introduction to Richard Koch's book says that while the 80:20 principle is well-known and influential, this work explains not only the theory but also how to put it to practical use. It is, the book jacket maintains, '…the key to controlling our lives' and it will enable us to 'leverage our efforts to multiply effectiveness'.

And to complete the circle

There is a wave of books that argue against specific fads. For example, there are two books out by Harvey Robbins and Michael Finley, entitled 'Why Change Doesn't Work' and 'Why Teams Don't Work'.

We don't know what the future holds, but we predict a few simple things:

1   Gurus and fads are not going to disappear. There is an emotional need for others to confirm what we believe, especially if they are experts or their ideas are set out in a potted form that makes it look logical and simple.

2   The trend towards anti-fads will continue. We shall have 'The Death of Empowerment', or 'Quality as a Non-management Issue'.

3   Fads will always be based around some mix of teams, empowerment, openness, communication, review, analysis and action; these are certain winners and are used in every aspect of positive management.

4   Old and passé fads will make a comeback. 'Management by Objectives', developed decades ago by Peter Drucker, is unfashionable now. It will rise Phoenix-like from the ashes and appear as the cornerstone of some new (but not so new) fad.

5   One area where a fad is due is in decentralised control. Something around giving middle and junior managers more executive authority over real management issues like budgets, hiring and firing and other such areas could well take off. It is a normal and desirable approach, to making managers more

managerial, but it seems to need a catchy title and a book of wisdom written about it... something like 'Managing upwards'.

Whatever the future holds, if a fad helps you make progress, ignore the flak and go for it. But please always remember that a fad is really only as good as the underlying themes and concepts that have been distilled from a set of theories or a much longer and wider work on what makes organisations work. Make sure you widen the viewfinder before you take the snapshot.

Bibliography

Why Teams Don't Work and Why Change Doesn't Work Harvey Robbins & Michael Finley, Orion Business Books, London 1997

The 80/20 Principle Richard Koch. Pub. Nicholas Brealey, London, 1997

Executive EQ: Emotional Intelligence in Business Robert Cooper & Ayman Sawaf, Orion Business Books, London 1997

Hawksmere publishing

Hawksmere publishes a wide range of books, reports, special briefings, psychometric tests and videos. Listed below is a selection of key titles.

Desktop Guides

The company director's desktop guide *David Martin • £39.99*

The company secretary's desktop guide *Roger Mason • £39.99*

The credit controller's desktop guide *Roger Mason • £39.99*

The finance and accountancy desktop guide
Ralph Tiffin • £39.99

The marketing strategy desktop guide *Norton Paley • £39.99*

The sales manager's desktop guide
Mike Gale and Julian Clay • £39.99

Masters in Management

Mastering business planning and strategy *Paul Elkin • £29.99*

Mastering financial management *Stephen Brookson • £29.99*

Mastering leadership *Michael Williams • £29.99*

Mastering marketing *Ian Ruskin-Brown • £29.99*

Mastering negotiations *Eric Evans • £29.99*

Mastering people management *Mark Thomas • £29.99*

Mastering personal and interpersonal skills
Peter Haddon • £29.99

Mastering project management *Cathy Lake • £29.99*

Essential Guides

The essential guide to buying and
selling unquoted businesses   *Ian Smith* • £29.99

The essential guide to business planning and raising finance
                    Naomi Langford-Wood and Brian Salter • £29.99

Business Action Pocketbooks

Edited by David Irwin

Building your business pocketbook	£10.99
Developing yourself and your staff pocketbook	£10.99
Finance and profitability pocketbook	£10.99
Managing and employing people pocketbook	£10.99
Sales and marketing pocketbook	£10.99
Managing projects and operations pocketbook	£9.99
Effective business communications pocketbook	£9.99
PR techniques that work	*Edited by Jim Dunn* • £9.99
Adair on leadership	*Edited by Neil Thomas* • £9.99

Other titles

The John Adair handbook of management and leadership
                                Edited by Neil Thomas • £29.95

The inside track to successful management
                                Dr Gerald Kushel • £16.95

The pension trustee's handbook (2nd edition)
                                Robin Ellison • £25

Boost your company's profits   *Barrie Pearson* • £12.99

Negotiate to succeed   *Julie Lewthwaite* • £12.99

The management tool kit   *Sultan Kermally* • £10.99

Working smarter   *Graham Roberts-Phelps* • £15.99

Test your management skills   *Michael Williams* • £12.99

The art of headless chicken management
                          Elly Brewer and Mark Edwards • £6.99

Exploiting IT in business   *David Irwin* • £12.99

EMU challenge and change – the implications for business
                                            John Atkin • £11.99

Everything you need for an NVQ in management
                                     Julie Lewthwaite • £19.99

Time management and personal development
                          John Adair and Melanie Allen • £9.99

Sales management and organisation   *Peter Green* • £9.99

Telephone tactics   *Graham Roberts-Phelps* • £9.99

Business health check   *Carol O' Connor* • £12.99

Companies don't succeed – people do!
                                Graham Roberts-Phelps • £12.99

Customer relationship management
                                Graham Roberts-Phelps • £12.99

Hawksmere also has an extensive range of reports and special
briefings which are written specifically for professionals wanting
expert information.

For a full listing of all Hawksmere publications, or to order any
title, please call Hawksmere Customer Services on 020 7824 8257
or fax your details on 020 7730 4293.